ISO/IEC 20000:2011
A POCKET GUIDE

ISO/IEC 20000:2011
A Pocket Guide

Colophon

Title:	ISO/IEC 20000:2011 – A Pocket Guide
Author:	Mart Rovers
Editor:	Jane Chittenden
Publisher:	Van Haren Publishing, Zaltbommel, www.vanharen.net
ISBN hardcopy:	978 90 8753 726 5
ISBN eBook:	978 90 8753 787 6
Print:	First edition, first impression, February 2012
	First edition, second impression, July 2012
	Second edition, first impression, February 2013
Design and Layout:	CO2 Premedia bv, Amersfoort – NL
Copyright:	© Van Haren Publishing 2013

For any further enquiries about Van Haren Publishing, please send an e-mail to: info@vanharen.net

Acknowledgements

We would like to thank the team of experts who contributed in such a major way to this publication. They have spent much time and kindly given their expertise to encourage better practices and understanding worldwide.

First of all we would like to thank Author Mart Rovers for pulling together the structure, approach and text. Always professional and knowledgeable, his kindness and humour means that he is indeed a great pleasure to work with. We are very privileged to work with Mart.

We also wish to thank the international team of experts who have reviewed the manuscript. These respected global experts have been kind enough to spend hours reviewing the title and sharing their hard-won expertise with the rest of the community. Always positive and professional these experts demonstrate the true strengths that can be found within IT Service Management.

Team:
Ashfaque Chowdhury	CIO, New Breed Logistics
Lynda Cooper	ISO20000 Evangelist, ITIL Master
Frederik van Eeden	Trainer and ISO20000 consultant
Subrata Guha	Director IT Services, UL DQS
Doug Houle	DHL
Wolfgang Moser	Consultant and Trainer, Prozess Delta
David W Nottingam	Manager - Configuration, Change, and Release Management, Premier, Inc.
Tony Powell	CIO, Florida Department of Revenue
Marc Taillefer	Consultant, Trainer and Coach in Management of IT Service

Kathy Tamer   Vice President & Chief Information
                     Officer - Retired, United Space Alliance

Paul R. Theisen,   Director of Information Services, NPL
                     Construction Company

Bryon Zimpfer   Change & Configuration Management,
                     Adobe Systems Inc.

Foreword

The aim of ISO/IEC 20000 is to provide a common reference
standard for any enterprise offering IT services to internal or
external customers. In 2004, when Van Haren Publishing first
produced a pocket book on the predecessors of this reference
standard, the world was already highly inter-connected.
Since then enterprises have taken even further strides to take
advantage of the benefits of global relationships. This makes the
need to embed a common set of terms and references within IT
even more desirable -- as the IT Advisory Board to Van Haren
Publishing we therefore welcome this new edition.

Any standard, in itself, will make no difference unless is
understood and applied wisely and appropriately by those
in the industry. As such we welcome this pocket guide which
presents the standard in an easily digestible format that can be
referenced easily. We believe it will be useful not only to experts
within the area of IT service management but also by business
managers and audit personnel who need to understand the
basic objective of this standard. This title supports the standard
which is intended to help businesses achieve their IT-enabled
business objectives and their IT quality and service management
objectives.

Members of Van Haren Publishing IT Advisory Board
Jacques Cazemier, VKA NL
Bill Hefley, University of Pittsburgh and ITSqc, LLC
Kevin Holland, NHS Connecting for Health
Brian Johnson, CA
David Jones, Pink Elephant UK
Alan Nance, Independent

Eric Rozemeijer, Quint Wellington Redwood
Gad J Selig, University of Bridgeport
Abbas Shahim, Atos Consulting
John Stewart, Independent

Contents

1 Introduction

1.1 Purpose of this book

The purpose of this book is to provide an easy to read document that explains the nature, the context, the purpose and interpretation of ISO/IEC 20000-1:2011 and ISO/IEC 20000-2:2012. It should bring ISO/IEC 20000, the international Information Technology Service Management (ITSM) standard, within reach of a rapidly growing global audience at a higher pace by providing an easy, accessible guide:

- To promote the awareness and the applicability of ISO/IEC 20000 as a valuable standard for service providers in the Information Technology (IT) industry;
- To support ISO/IEC 20000 adoption, application and compliance initiatives, training, accreditation and certification;
- To produce an easy to use interpretation of the core content of ISO/IEC 20000-1:2011 and ISO/IEC 20000-2:2012 for any IT professional interested in the design and delivery of quality IT services;
- To provide guidance when implementing and improving ITSM even when ISO/IEC 20000 certification is not the end goal.

"ISO/IEC 20000 - A Pocket Guide" is aimed at a broad range of IT professionals who are looking for guidance and direction to improve IT service quality. In addition, this book is aimed at customers and consumers of IT services who wish to gain insight into what they can expect from a service provider and for ways to distinguish between different service providers providing the same services.

The contents of this book along with the standard may be applied:

- When at the very beginning of your ITSM journey, in particular when seeking a measuring stick to objectively visualize improvements or when seeking a compass to steer you towards your intended service improvement goals and objectives
- When looking for ways to boost your (stalled) ITSM adoption initiative, in particular when ITSM successes are hard to quantify and qualify or when momentum is (about to be) lost
- When looking for ways to continuously improve your levels of IT process efficiency and effectiveness, your service quality levels and your customer satisfaction levels

1.2   Structure of this book

The book starts with an introduction to ISO/IEC 20000 by describing its nature and purpose (this chapter). This covers the structure, the history, and the purpose of ISO/IEC 20000, as well as the standard's contributions and who will benefit from it. Chapter 2 provides an overview of the standard.

The following two chapters address the environment of ISO/IEC 20000 by putting it in context. Chapter 3 explains how ISO standards are developed. Chapter 4 explains the meaning of accreditation, certification, assessments, audits, scoping and applicability.

The remaining chapters cover the interpretation of the standard. This involves the relations with the Information Technology Infrastructure Library® (ITIL®) and Risk Management; the alignment with ISO 9001 and ISO/IEC 27001 (Chapter 5); communications requirements for the service provider

(Chapter 6); and a description of the ISO/IEC 20000-1:2011 requirements, together with a self-assessment approach (Chapter 7 and Chapter 8). The standard's definitions of its terminology are provided in appendix A. The changes between the 2005 and the 2011 version of the ISO/IEC 20000-1 standard are listed in appendix B. Annex C covers a brief explanation of ISO/IEC 20000-2:2012.

This book does not provide a copy of the ISO/IEC 20000-1:2011 or ISO/IEC 20000-2:2012 standard. For this we refer to Van Haren's book *ISO/IEC 20000 – An Introduction*[1], or to the ISO organization. The ISO/IEC 20000 publications can be obtained from ISO (http://www.iso.org/iso/store.htm). However, this book does describe each ISO/IEC 20000-1:2011 requirement in the author's language and interpretation of it. Organizations who are seeking certification are recommended to obtain a formal copy of the standard to benefit from these interpretations. Certification audits will be based on the official standard and not this book.

Neither does the book describe the implementation steps to be considered when attempting to adhere to the standard. For this we refer to Van Haren's book *ISO/IEC 20000 – An Implementation Roadmap*[2]. This book does, however, include helpful guidance with interpreting and understanding the standard's requirements to allow for a more rapid adherence.

---

1 At the time this book was written, the available ISO/IEC 20000 – An Introduction book was still based on the 2005 version of ISO/IEC 20000.
2 At the time this book was written, the available ISO/IEC 20000 – An Implementation Roadmap book was still based on the 2005 version of ISO/IEC 20000.

1.3   Audience for this book

This book is written for IT professionals who are seeking ways to improve their organization's:

1. Efficiency, effectiveness, and/or performance in general, including the delivery of services and the supporting processes
2. Service quality levels' predictability, consistency and repeatability
3. Attitude, behavior, culture and move from a technology focus towards a more end-to-end service and customer focus
4. Communication processes, including those affecting the customers, the users, the service provider's staff, and the suppliers
5. Information and knowledge gathering and collaboration in support of a higher quality and informed decision-making process
6. Transparency, including value creation and delivery, resource utilization and demands, cost management, and risk management
7. Continual improvement of service quality in alignment with customer needs and market opportunities
8. Ability to determine objectively its current service quality level by comparing its service quality levels with an international auditable standard specific for IT, including setting a baseline and benchmarking against comparable service providers in the same industry segment
9. Ability to determine the direction and the steps involving improvement efforts addressing higher service quality levels and higher customer satisfaction

The target audience for this book is purposely described in broad terms. The ISO/IEC 20000 standard is beneficial to every IT professional. Whether you are in an IT leadership, practitioner, advisory, analyst, instructor or auditor role, the standard provides guidance and direction towards quality IT services across the IT organization and IT industry. Limiting the target audience would unnecessarily impair the standard's reputation, potential and applicability.

2 Overview of ISO/IEC 20000

This chapter introduces ISO/IEC 20000. It outlines the structure of ISO/IEC 20000, its history, and its purpose; and explains the contributions and benefits of the standard to IT organizations.

2.1 The ISO/IEC 20000 Series

The core of the ISO/IEC 20000 standard consists of several documents:

1. ISO/IEC 20000-1:2011 **Service management system requirements**. This is the formal specification of the standard. It describes the required activities, documents and records defined in 256 'shall' statements.

2. ISO/IEC 20000-2 **Guidance on the application of service management systems** describes the best practices in detail and provides guidance to auditors and recommendations for service providers planning for service improvements defined in 'should' statements.

3. ISO/IEC TR[1] 20000-3 **Guidance on scope definition and applicability of ISO/IEC 20000-1** provides guidance on determining the scope of certification and the applicability of the standard.

4. ISO/IEC TR 20000-4 **Process Reference Model** facilitates the development of a process assessment model that will be described in ISO/IEC TR 15504-8 **Information Technology – Process Assessment**.

---

1 TR: Technical Report

5. ISO/IEC TR 20000-5 **Exemplar Implementation Plan for
    ISO/IEC 20000-1** provides guidance on the implementation
    of the standard's requirements.

Other parts of the standard are currently being planned.

More details of each document will be described in the upcoming
chapters.

2.2   History of ISO/IEC 20000

The IT Infrastructure Library (ITIL) is accepted all over the
world as a de facto reference for best practice processes in IT
Service Management. Inherently, because ITIL is a framework
and not a standard, showing compliance with ITIL is impossible
for service providers[2]. This changed in the year 2000 when a
formally documented standard became available. It was BSI
(the British Standards Institution) who officially determined the
requirements for the effective delivery of services to the business
and its customers in a British Standard: BS 15000.

The first edition of BS 15000 was published in November 2000,
based on an earlier publication - DISC PD0005: 1998 - the
Code of Practice for IT Service Management. BS 15000-1:2002
became the second edition, which was the result of experience
and feedback from early adopters of the first edition. The
development of a certification strategy gave a major boost to the
acceptance of BS 15000 as a formal standard.

---

2 Note that for some frameworks defined assessment methods do exist.
   An example is SCAMPI for an assessment against CMMI.

On 15 December 2005, ISO, the International Organization for Standardization, accepted BS 15000 as an international ISO standard: ISO/IEC 20000:2005, the first edition of the standard.

There are two ways to create an ISO standard:
1. A cooperative creation by involved countries, or
2. The fast-track route based upon a national standard.

For the acceptation of this British Standard, ISO followed the fast-track route. Preceding its acceptance as an ISO standard, BS 15000 was already copied and accepted in the national standards bodies of Australia and South Africa.

More information about the ISO organization, its processes and procedures can be found in Chapter 3.

Besides ITIL, many IT Service Management frameworks are available. Some are public domain and freely available and others can be acquired at a fee or cost. Furthermore, several vendors have developed their own framework in support of their IT Service Management solutions and offerings. It is a misperception that ISO/IEC 20000 is solely based on ITIL or that the adoption of ITIL is a prerequisite to comply with the requirements of ISO/IEC 20000. A service provider is free to choose the IT Service Management framework, or a combination of frameworks, that it prefers in support of its endeavors to benefit from the standard. ITIL is not known for its strengths in areas like IT governance, project and program management, risk management, information security management, quality management, and business analysis. These are areas for which widely accepted complementary frameworks and standards exist, all contributing to becoming ISO/IEC 20000 certified as a service provider.

The first edition of the standard, ISO/IEC 20000:2005, in particular the Specification, ISO/IEC 20000-1:2005, was a slightly adapted version of BS 15000-1. The BS 15000 Code of Practice (BS 15000-2) was upgraded to ISO/IEC 20000-2 (Code of Practice) on December 15, 2005. In late 2011 or early 2012 the new edition is expected on this document.

ISO/IEC 20000-1:2005, the **Specification**, was the formal specification of the standard's initial release. It described the required activities defined in 170 'shall' statements.

Part Two of the standard, ISO/IEC 20000-2:2005, the **Code of Practice**, provides guidance and recommendations for the interpretation of the requirements of ISO/IEC 20000-1. It provides guidance to auditors and offers assistance to service providers who are planning service improvements. It lists guidelines and suggestions that service providers 'should' address when wishing to be audited against the ISO/IEC 20000-1 requirements and become certified. The Code of Practice is not part of the requirements. It supports the efforts to meet the requirements described in ISO/IEC 20000-1.

Three additional parts of the standard, parts 3, 4 and 5, have been released in 2009 and 2010 as described in section 2.1.

There are three parts of the standard that have yet to be released: ISO/IEC 20000-6, -7, and -8.

The diagram below depicts the relationship between part 1 and part 2 of the ISO/IEC 20000 standard and the many ITSM frameworks available in the market:

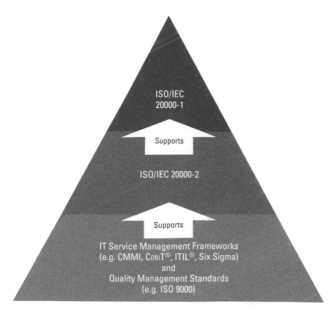

Figure 2.1 Relationship between ISO/IEC 20000 part 1 and 2 and ITSM frameworks

The second edition of the standard, ISO/IEC 20000-1:2011 **Service management system requirements**, was released on April 15, 2011. It describes the required activities defined in 256 'shall' statements. The reasons for publishing a new version of the standard were:

- All ISO standards must be reviewed every five years; this is an ISO requirement

- Comments deferred from the ISO/IEC 2000:2005 publication have been addressed in this new version
- Many improvements have been suggested over the years
- The Joint Technical Committee of ISO responsible for the standard has grown to more than 20 countries; this increase in popularity has resulted in many suggestions for improvements
- A closer alignment with ISO 9001, the Quality Management standard
- The publication of ITILv3 in 2007
- A closer alignment with ISO/IEC 27001, the Information Security Management standard
- A stronger emphasis of interfaces between processes
- Improved consistency of international ITSM terminology

The benefits of the new version of the standard are:
- Easier integration with Management Systems of standards such as ISO 9001 and ISO/IEC 27001
- Improved clarity of interpretation of requirements
- Improved clarity of terminology
- Increased quality, consistency, and productivity of service delivery due to the additional requirements of ISO/IEC 20000:2011 compared to the 2005 edition

More information about the main differences between the 2005 and the 2011 edition of the standard is addressed in Appendix B.

Transition for Certified Organizations
Organizations who are already certified and wish to move to the 2011 edition of the standard should discuss the timescales with their Registered Certification Body.

2.3   Purpose of ISO/IEC 20000

The purpose of ISO/IEC 20000 is to provide a common reference standard for any enterprise offering IT services to internal or external customers.

Given that communication plays an essential role in IT Service Management[3], one of the most important goals of the standard is to create a common terminology for service providers, their suppliers and their customers.

The standard promotes the adoption of an integrated process approach for the management of IT services. With a high number of the standard's requirements referring to process integration or process interfaces, a strong emphasis is given to this "*integrated process approach*"[4]. By making process integration such high

---

3   Examples of confusion created by unclear definitions of terminology used in the IT industry are:
• What is the difference between the severity and the priority of an incident?
• What is the difference between a problem, an incident, an event and a service request?
• What is the difference between response time and resolution time and how is each being measured?

By clearly defining the terminology and consistently using the right terminology confusion can be avoided when the parties involved communicate with each other. Avoiding confusion will increase the service provider's trust levels.

4   Integrated process approach is verbiage straight from the standard. By emphasizing on the importance of process integration, the standard in essence is requiring cooperation and communication between the parties involved in the Management System (e.g. customers, suppliers, and the service provider's staff) and as such promoting the principles of a value network. Processes never operate stand-alone and therefore interface with other processes. For example Change Management has strong interfaces with Release and Deployment Management. Since many parties are involved with both processes, the process interfaces point out the required cooperation and communication between the parties.

priority the standard inherently makes communication play a central role in enabling effective IT Service Management.

The standard's processes have been positioned in a process model, representing the minimal activities mandatory for quality IT Service Management - things that are common to and required by every service provider. ISO/IEC 20000 does not address local requirements or specific regulatory or statutory requirements, although the standard requires that these are considered in the service requirements.

ISO/IEC 20000 represents a set of minimum requirements to audit an organization against effective IT Service Management. The standard has enabled service providers globally to determine formal compliance to these IT Service Management requirements. This formal compliance can be accomplished through independent and external auditors or Registered Certification Bodies (RCBs). RCBs are registered with a national accreditation body. Many of the national accreditation bodies are registered with the International Accreditation Forum (IAF).

Furthermore, the standard contributes to the delivery and support of quality services by the service provider enabled by a Service Management System (SMS) that is based on the eight principles of Quality Management as defined in ISO 9000. These principles, along with examples of ISO/IEC 20000 requirements, are listed in the table below:

Table 2.1 Quality Management Principles

Quality Management Principle	ISO/IEC 20000 requirement (examples)
Customer focus	Planning for the new or changed services shall be agreed with the customer.
Leadership	Top management shall provide evidence of its commitment to planning, establishing, implementing, operating, monitoring, reviewing, maintaining, and improving the SMS and the services.
Involvement of people	The service provider's personnel performing work affecting conformity to service requirements shall be competent on the basis of appropriate education, training, skills and experience.
Process approach	The service provider shall implement and operate the SMS for the design, transition, delivery and improvement of services according to the Service Management plan, through activities including the management of Service Management processes.
System approach to management	The service provider shall establish and maintain documents, including records, to ensure effective planning, operation and control of the SMS; this includes policies and objectives of Service Management, a Service Management plan, process policies and plans, a catalog of services and service level agreements (SLAs), and Service Management processes and procedures.
Continual improvement	There shall be a policy on continual improvement of the SMS and the services.
Factual approach to decision making	The service provider shall make decisions and take actions based on the findings in service reports.
Mutually beneficial supplier relationships	The service provider shall agree with the supplier service levels to support and align with the SLAs between the service provider and the customer.

By meeting the requirements of the ISO/IEC 20000 standard, the service provider has incorporated these quality principles ensuring the delivery and support of quality services.

More information about the standard's SMS can be found in Appendix B.

2.4   Contributions and benefits

ISO/IEC 20000 contributions

The ISO/IEC 20000 standard is being adopted globally by hundreds of companies and organizations[5]. Many service providers operating in a commercial environment are using the certification as a marketing advantage. Others are using the standard as a vehicle to show their customers that quality services are important to them. Below is a list of situations where the use of the ISO/IEC 20000 standard can provide a valuable contribution.

- For customers who are comparing service providers: ISO/IEC 20000 provides uniform and common language as well as a standard for benchmarking
- For customers who are selecting a service provider: an ISO/IEC 20000 certified service provider can express added value when offering its services and can distinguish itself from its competition
- For customers or service providers who are looking for an independent and non-biased baseline to measure the service provider's performance against and use this baseline as a norm

---

5   By mid-2011, about 700 companies worldwide were ISO/IEC 20000 certified through the APMG certification scheme. Yet there are many other schemes around the world, but numbers are not available.

- For customers and service providers who are looking for a norm for reliable and available quality services
- For customers and service providers who are looking for ways to shorten the time-to-market of their products and/or services
- For customers and service providers who are seeking for increased transparency of costs of service provisioning and of total cost of ownership (TCO) and the associated risks
- For service providers who are looking for ways to better understand the needs of the customer. ISO/IEC 20000 can be a norm to improve IT governance
- For service providers who are looking for ways to boost their professional image and increase staff morale
- For service providers who desire to become more responsive and shorten their response times in response to their customer's needs
- For service providers who need guidance on determining which IT Service Management best practices to focus on first
- For service providers who are adopting industry best practices to improve the effectiveness and efficiency of their performance
- For service providers who are in need of a "tool" to initiate, revitalize and/or boost an IT Service Management improvement endeavor
- For service providers who are looking for ways to implement changes faster and more effectively
- For service providers who need alignment between a broad range of quality improvement to be implemented in parallel
- For service providers who are looking for ways to improve their sourcing success rate through well-aligned process interfaces and common and consistent language

- For suppliers who are looking for a better alignment of their services and processes with their customer's services and processes

Most Service Providers meeting the ISO/IEC 20000 requirements have experienced higher customer satisfaction, an improved service quality an increase in process efficiency and IT professionalism.

ISO/IEC 20000 benefits

There are many benefits of being certified or simply using the standard even when not seeking certification. Below are a few examples.

- To qualify for new customers: more and more companies and organizations consider ISO/IEC 20000 certification an essential requirement for conducting business with a new vendor or supplier
- To enter global markets: the ISO/IEC 20000 standards are widely recognized
- To objectively measure compliance with an international quality standard for ITSM
- To have better information available for numerous purposes
- To streamline various process improvements that may go on simultaneously in the service provider's organization
- To provide guidance on prioritizing the best practices to be implemented
- To give a service provider a competitive edge
- To show a drive for quality services
- To objectively assess and benchmark the service provider's level of maturity

- To increase customer focus and transparency of value provided to the business
- To establish a culture of continual improvement in IT
- To boost the morale and professional image of the service provider's staff

Benefiting IT disciplines

IT Service Management practices encompass all areas in the service provider's organization. To underline this characteristic some refer to it as end-to-end IT Service Management. Given that ITSM "touches" every part of the service provider's organization, it is therefore to be expected that meeting the ISO/IEC 20000 requirements is a combined effort by multiple IT disciplines. In order to define, design, implement, maintain and improve quality services, a combination and coherent set of multiple perspectives is crucial. These perspectives are often combined into the people, processes and technology aspects of a service. The table below shows several examples of service perspectives for each service aspect.

Table 2.2 Service aspects and service perspectives

Service Perspectives:	People	Process	Technology
Service Aspects:	Knowledge, skills, and experience	Process policies	Architectures
	Attitude, behavior, and culture	Process descriptions	Process automation
	Management style	Procedures	Information systems
	Organizational structure	Work instructions	Equipment
	Incentives	Methods	Management tools
		Techniques	
		Templates	

Given this breadth and depth of IT Service Management, the implementation of ISO/IEC 20000-1 requires the involvement of multiple disciplines in IT. While not attempting to be complete, a list of common IT disciplines is provided below, along with examples of ISO/IEC 20000 requirements that are usually addressed in the respective discipline.

Table 2.3 IT disciplines benefiting from implementing the ISO/IEC 20000 requirements

IT disciplines which will benefit ISO/IEC 20000	ISO/IEC 20000 requirement (examples)
Business Analysis	• The service provider shall identify the service requirements for the new or changed services. • New or changed services shall be planned to fulfill the service requirements. • Planning for the new or changed services shall be agreed with the customer and interested parties. • As input to planning, the service provider shall take into consideration the potential financial, organizational, and technical impact of delivering the new or changed services.
Communication Management	• Top management shall communicate the importance of fulfilling service requirements. • The Service Management policy shall be communicated and understood by the service provider's personnel. • Documented procedures for communication shall be established and implemented.
Document Management	• The service provider shall establish and maintain documents, including records, to ensure effective planning, operation and control of the SMS. • A documented procedure, including the authorities and responsibilities, shall be established to define the document management controls

IT disciplines which will benefit ISO/IEC 20000	ISO/IEC 20000 requirement (examples)
	• A documented procedure shall be established to define the controls needed for the identification, storage, protection, retrieval, retention and disposal of records.
Human Resource Management	• The service provider's personnel performing work affecting conformity to service requirements shall be competent on the basis of appropriate education, training, skills and experience. • The service provider shall ensure that its personnel are aware of how they contribute to the achievement of Service Management objectives and the fulfillment of service requirements • The service provider shall maintain appropriate records of education, training, skills and experience.
IT Governance	• The service provider shall demonstrate governance of processes operated by other parties • Plans created for specific processes shall be aligned with the Service Management plan. • The service provider shall demonstrate accountability for the processes and authority to require adherence to the processes. • Top management shall provide evidence of its commitment to planning, establishing, implementing, operating, monitoring, reviewing, maintaining, and improving the SMS and the services. • The service provider shall manage improvement activities that include setting targets for improvements in one or more of quality, value, capability, cost, productivity, resource utilization and risk reduction.
Knowledge Management	• The service provider shall determine the necessary competence for personnel. • The service provider's personnel performing work affecting conformity to service requirements shall be competent on the basis of appropriate education, training, skills and experience.

IT disciplines which will benefit ISO/IEC 20000	ISO/IEC 20000 requirement (examples)
	• The Service Management plan shall contain human, technical, information and financial resources necessary to achieve the Service Management objectives. • The service provider shall implement and operate the SMS for the design, transition, delivery and improvement of services according to the Service Management plan, through activities including the management of human, technical and information resources. • Management reviews shall include current and forecast human, technical, information and financial resource levels. • The service provider shall ensure that personnel involved in the incident and request management process can access and use relevant information.
Management of Change	• Top management shall appoint a member of the service provider's management who has the authorities and responsibilities that include ensuring that activities are performed to identify, document and fulfill service requirements. • The capacity plan shall include the potential impact of statutory, regulatory, contractual or organizational changes. • Planning for new or changed services shall include authorities and responsibilities for design, development and transition activities, activities to be performed by the service provider and other parties including activities across interfaces from the service provider to other parties, communication to interested parties, timescales for planned activities, and the identification, assessment and management of risks.

IT disciplines which will benefit ISO/IEC 20000	ISO/IEC 20000 requirement (examples)
Portfolio Management	• The Service Management scope shall be defined by the name of the organizational unit providing the services, and the services to be delivered. • The service provider shall review outputs from the planning and design activities for new or changed services against the agreed service requirements. • Planning for the new or changed services shall be agreed with the customer and interested parties. • The service provider shall agree a catalog of services with the customer.
Project and Program Management	• The service provider shall use the design and transition of new or changed services process for all new services and changes to services with the potential to have a major impact on services or the customer. • Assessment, approval, scheduling and reviewing of new or changed services shall be controlled by the change management process. • Planning for the new or changed services shall contain authorities and responsibilities for design, development and transition activities, activities to be performed by the service provider and other parties including activities across interfaces from the service provider to other parties, timescales for planned activities, dependencies on other services, testing required for the new or changed services, service acceptance criteria, and expected outcomes from delivering the new or changed services, expressed in measurable terms
Quality Management	• Planning for the new or changed services shall be agreed with the customer • Top management shall provide evidence of its commitment to planning, establishing, implementing, operating, monitoring, reviewing, maintaining, and improving the SMS and the services

IT disciplines which will benefit ISO/IEC 20000	ISO/IEC 20000 requirement (examples)
	• The service provider's personnel performing work affecting conformity to service requirements shall be competent on the basis of appropriate education, training, skills and experience • There shall be a policy on continual improvement of the SMS and the services.
Strategic Risk Management	• Top management shall ensure that risks to services are assessed and managed. • The Service Management plan shall contain an approach to be taken for the management of risks and the criteria for accepting risks. • Activities to implement and operate the SMS include the identification, assessment and management of risks to the services. • The input to management reviews shall include information on risks. • The service provider shall manage improvement activities that include setting targets for improvements in one or more of quality, value, capability, cost, productivity, resource utilization and risk reduction.

What we can learn from this table is that implementing the ISO/IEC 20000 requirements is done throughout the service provider's organization. Many departments and teams in the organization will contribute to meeting what is required by the standard. Furthermore, when determining where to find evidence in the service provider's organization of meeting the standard's requirements, often the organization is already practicing what the standard requires, but maybe not in a formalized way. Such practices jumpstart the overall compliance efforts.

3 Development of ISO standards[1]

ISO/IEC 20000 is managed by the International Organization for Standardization (ISO). ISO is a network of the national standards institutes of more than 150 countries, on the basis of one member per country, with a Central Secretariat in Geneva, Switzerland, that coordinates the system. More than 20 countries were involved with the development of ISO/IEC 20000, during mid-2011. ISO is the world's largest developer of standards.

ISO standards are developed through defined processes including several pre-defined stages in order to create an industry-wide consensus. ISO standards are developed according to the following principles:

- Consensus:
  The views of all stakeholders are taken into account
- Industry wide:
  The solutions provided satisfy industries and customers worldwide
- Voluntary:
  International standardization is market driven and therefore based on voluntary involvement of all interests in the marketplace.

The three main phases in the development process of ISO standards are:
1. Once the need for an International Standard, expressed by an industry sector, has been recognized and formally agreed,

---

1 Portions of this chapter's text is taken from ISO's website (www.iso.org).

the first phase involves definition of the technical scope of the future standard. This phase is usually carried out in working groups which comprise technical experts from countries interested in the subject matter.

2. Once agreement has been reached on which technical aspects are to be covered in the standard, a second phase is entered during which countries negotiate the detailed specifications within the standard. This is the consensus-building phase.

3. The final phase comprises the formal approval of the resulting draft International Standard (the acceptance criteria stipulate approval by two-thirds of the ISO members that have participated actively in the standards development process, and approval by 75 percent of all members who vote), following which the agreed text is published as an ISO International Standard.

Currently, there are over 18,000 international standards held by the ISO organization.

International Standards are developed by ISO technical committees (TC) and subcommittees (SC) by a six-step process:

Stage 1: Proposal stage
- During this stage the need for a standard is determined and either accepted or rejected through a voting process

Stage 2: Preparatory stage
- During this consensus-building phase the TC/SC sets up a working group of experts led by a project leader which develops a draft version

Stage 3: Committee stage
- As soon as a first draft version is available it is registered by the ISO Central Secretariat. It is distributed for comments

and consensus is reached on the technical content. A Draft
International Standard (DIS) version is then submitted.

Stage 4: Enquiry stage

- During this stage the DIS is circulated to all ISO member
  bodies for voting and comment, within a period of five
  months. It is approved for submission as a Final Draft
  International Standard (FDIS) if a two-thirds majority of
  the members of the TC/SC is in favor and not more than
  one-quarter of the total number of votes cast are negative. If
  the approval criteria are not met, the text is returned to the
  originating TC/SC for further study and a revised document
  will again be circulated for voting and comment as a draft
  International Standard.

Stage 5: Approval stage

- The FDIS is circulated to all ISO member bodies by the
  ISO Central Secretariat for a final Yes/No vote within a
  period of two months. If technical comments are received
  during this period, they are no longer considered at this
  stage, but registered for consideration during a future
  revision of the International Standard. The text is approved
  as an International Standard if a two-thirds majority of the
  members of the TC/SC is in favor and not more than one-
  quarter of the total number of votes cast are negative. If these
  approval criteria are not met, the standard is referred back
  to the originating TC/SC for reconsideration in light of the
  technical reasons submitted in support of the negative votes
  received.

Stage 6: Publication stage

- Once a final draft International Standard has been approved,
  only minor editorial changes, if and where necessary, are
  introduced into the final text. The final text is sent to the

ISO Central Secretariat which publishes the International Standard.

Review

- All International Standards are reviewed within three years after publication and then every five years after the first review by all the ISO member bodies. A majority of the members of the TC/SC decides whether an International Standard should be confirmed, revised or withdrawn.

Besides standards, ISO also produces other documents such as Publicly Available Specifications (PAS), Guides, Technical Specifications (TS), Technical Reports (TR) and International Workshop Agreements (IWA). ISO/IEC 20000 examples are:

- ISO/IEC TR 20000-3 Guidance on scope definition and applicability of ISO/IEC 20000-1
- ISO/IEC TR 20000-4 Process reference model
- ISO/IEC TR 20000-5 Exemplar implementation plan

The procedures for developing ISO standards are defined in the ISO/IEC (International Electro-technical Committee) Directives and ISO supplement. There are three core documents describing basic procedural and drafting rules to be followed by ISO committees. These three documents are:

- ISO/IEC Directives, Part 1: Procedures for the technical work
- ISO Supplement, Procedures specific to ISO
- ISO/IEC Directives, Part 2: Rules for the structure and drafting of International Standards

ISO/IEC Joint Technical Committee (JTC) 1 (Information technology) has adopted ISO/IEC Directives, Part 1 together with JTC 1 Supplement. More information can be found on ISO's website: www.iso.org.

4 Accreditation, certification and assessment

This chapter introduces accreditation (assessment for conformity and certification); lists the certification training schemes available and the institutions providing the qualification schemes; outlines the processes for assessing readiness for certification; and describes the certification process. Finally, this chapter explains the scope and applicability of the standard.

4.1 Accreditation

Organizations (that is, service providers) can be assessed for conformity with ISO/IEC 20000 and - if the assessment was positive - they can be certified by official Registered Certification Bodies (RCBs). RCBs need to get accreditation from an Accreditation Organization in a country that is a member of ISO.

Accredited RCBs follow the requirements of the ISO/IEC 17021:2011 standard: *"Conformity assessment — Requirements for bodies providing audit and certification of management systems"*. Certification Bodies (RCBs) are registered with and accredited by an Accreditation Body (AB).

An AB usually operates on a national level. There are over 40 national ABs who are members of the International Accreditation Forum (IAF), including ANAB (USA), CNAB (China), DAR (Germany), JAB (Japan) Accreditation Board for Conformity Assessment JAS-ANZ: JAS-ANZ Joint Australia and new Zealand), RvA (The Netherlands), SANAS (South Africa), SINCERT-FIDEA (Italy), UKAS (UK), and more.

The IAF (www.iaf.nu) is an association of organizations whose core business is to check and control the consistency of how audit companies actually do audits. In this context 'audit companies' are RCBs. Its primary function is to develop a single worldwide program of conformity assessment which reduces risk for business and its customers by assuring them that accredited certificates may be relied upon.

In an often combined effort, also ISO Geneva plays a role in overseeing the ABs.

RCBs are assessed and approved by the certification scheme owner, e.g. APM Group. RCBs will be screened thoroughly for independence and competence. RCB applications are accepted only when coming from Certification Bodies who are accredited by their relevant national accreditation body.

Figure 4.1 Accreditation and certification sequence

In sequence of events, the Accreditation Body accredits the Registered Certification Body and the latter certifies the service provider (Figure 4.1).

4.2   Certification training for individuals

The increase in number of IT Service Management implementations based on the ISO/IEC 20000 standard has resulted in several Examination Institutes around the globe introducing a variety of qualification schemes consisting of ISO/IEC 20000 certification training for individuals. In turn, these training courses have increased the awareness and competency, and have accelerated the rate of service providers benefiting from the standard, whether organizational certification is the end goal or not.

The table below lists, in alphabetical order, some of the qualification schemes available and the respective organizations owning the scheme. Certain schemes are offered through multiple Examination Institutes. For more information, including the accredited course providers offering the certification training courses in preparation for a certification examination, a link to their website is included.

Note that even though some examination titles carry the same name, or qualification schemes look alike, this does not imply that the examination format and duration or the associated course content and duration are the same. You are encouraged to do your due diligence before deciding on a training course of a course provider accredited by a particular Examination Institute.

Furthermore, some qualification schemes offer so-called side entries for students who already possess other IT Service Management certificates. Side-entries accelerate the advancement through the qualification scheme and expedite the process of obtaining higher-level certifications.

Table 4.1 Qualification schemes

Examination Institute	Beginners-level examinations	Advanced-level examinations	Auditor-level examinations
APMG www.apmg -international. com	Foundation	Practitioner	Auditor
BCS www.bcs.org	Foundation		
EXIN www.exin -exams.com	Foundation Foundation Bridge	*Professional-level:* • Support of IT Services • Control of IT Services • Management and Improvement of ITSM Processes • Delivery of IT Services • Alignment of IT and the Business • Associate Consultant/ Auditor *Expert-level:* • Consultant/Manager *Master-level:* • Executive Consultant/ Manager	Associate Consultant/ Auditor Internal Auditor
IRCA www.irca.org			Provisional Internal Auditor Internal Auditor Provisional Auditor Auditor Lead Auditor Principal Auditor

Examination Institute	Beginners-level examinations	Advanced-level examinations	Auditor-level examinations
PEOPLECERT GROUP www.peoplecert.org	Foundation	*Expert-level:* • Professional *Consultant-level:* • Junior Consultant • Consultant • Senior Consultant	Professional Auditor Internal Auditor Auditor Lead Auditor
RABQSA www.rabqsa.com			Internal Auditor Lead Auditor
TüV-SüD www.tuev-sued.com	Foundation Foundation Bridge	*Professional-level:* • Support of IT Services • Control of IT Services • Management and Improvement of ITSM Processes • Delivery of IT Services • Alignment of IT and the Business • Associate Consultant/ Auditor *Expert-level:* • Consultant/Manager *Master-level:* • Executive Consultant/ Manager	Associate Consultant/ Auditor Internal Auditor Executive Auditor

4.3   Assessments and audits

Before embarking on a full-scale certification audit, organizations seeking ISO/IEC 20000 certification are encouraged to assess their readiness for certification. The figure below displays several steps to consider before a certification audit, which is shown as the third party (external) audit by the RCB.

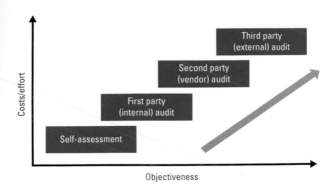

Figure 4.2 Assessing readiness for certification

1. A **self-assessment** is usually conducted by the service provider's staff, for example by the project team or by the Process Owners. In Chapter 8 some guidance is provided on conducting a self-assessment. The low costs involved with such self assessment allows for repeating this step frequently. However, when assessing your own work, the objectivity may not be very high. Self-assessments can easily be created by turning every "shall" statement into a question and by listing evidence for every requirement.

2. A **first party (internal) audit** is usually conducted by the service provider's audit department. Having someone other than a project team member or a Process Owner assessing the level of compliance increases the objectivity of the outcomes. This also implies that the internal auditors are familiar with not only the standard's requirements, but also with the basic concepts of IT Service Management. It is recommended that internal auditors without such background participate in ISO/IEC 20000 certification training courses to obtain this knowledge. There are various certification schemes available

in the market. More about those schemes is in section 4.2 above.

3. The **second party (vendor) audit** is usually conducted by a consulting firm with a strong background in IT Service Management implementations combined with experience preparing service providers for ISO/IEC 20000 certification and consultants who are certified to conduct internal audits.[1] Another option is to have an auditing firm conducting this audit, which is not the RCB who will conduct the certification audit, the third party (external) audit. Second party audits take longer than first party audits and self-assessment; they are more expensive, but also more objective.

4. The **third party (external) audits** are conducted by RCBs. Note that an RCB cannot be a company providing Service Management consultancy services because of the conflict of interest. An audit must be independent hence the need to separate audit from consultancy services. The third party (external) audit is described in greater detail in the next section.

A successful third party (external) audit is awarded with ISO/IEC 20000-1 certification. This means that the service provider complies with every requirement - that is, "shall", of the ISO/IEC 20000 standard. An organization does not become certified when missing out on meeting one or more requirement(s)[2].

---

1 Note that an audit of sub-contractors conducted by a service provider is also considered a second party audit.
2 Note that organizations with a few minor non-conformities do get certified.

Auditors look for two components of evidence:
1. Documents
2. Records

A **document** is used to describe information and its supporting medium. Information is in readable form and may include computer data. It is evidence of the service provider's intentions with regard to Service Management. Examples include policy statements, plans, process documents, procedure documents, service level agreements and contracts.

A **record** is used to describe documents stating results achieved or providing evidence of activities performed. Records function as evidence of activities, rather than evidence of intentions. Examples include audit reports, requests for change, incident reports, individual training records, meeting minutes, action item lists, log files, and invoices.

4.4   Certification

Although service providers can claim their compliance with the specifications of the ISO/IEC 20000 standard, a formal audit and certification will carry significantly more weight.

The certification process is usually a seven-step endeavor:
1. **Questionnaire**
   - The RCB will send a questionnaire to the service provider to answer questions referring to details about:
     a. The standard's requirements to be met; for example, certification can only be granted to one single legal entity and the service provider does not have to own the infrastructure that is going to be part of the audit

  b. The company; for example, the geographical locations and the size of the organization
- The response of the questionnaire provides the RCB with information that is needed to create and send a formal quote to the service provider

2. Application for Assessment

- Upon approval of the quote, an application form must be completed by the service provider and returned to the RCB
- An initial meeting with the lead auditor will be arranged
- The lead auditor will explain the assessment process
- The preliminary scoping statement[3] will be discussed and agreed upon
- An assessment date and audit program will be agreed

3. Optional Pre-audit

- A Pre-Audit is a high-level assessment to determine the current status of the company with regards to the ISO/IEC 20000 requirements
- A Pre-Audit will help the service provider's management to understand what is to be expected
- The auditor will point out areas of concern to reduce the risk of non-conformance during the actual audit

4. Initial Audit (stage 1)

- The following is determined during the Initial Audit:
  - a. Has the management system been implemented with controls which include:
    - The documentation of all policies?
    - The documentation of all processes and procedures?
  - b. The auditor will plan the Certification Audit
  - c. The final scoping statement will agreed upon

---

3 The Scope of Certification is explained in chapter 4.5.

    d. An initial assessment of the documentation of the management system and the process documents is conducted

- Deficiencies during this Initial Audit are called nonconformities or non-conformances[4]; these non-conformances will be added to a Corrective Action Plan (CAP)
- There are two types of nonconformities:
  - a. Minor nonconformity: A failure to meet one requirement of a clause
  - b. Major nonconformity: A number of minor nonconformities combined or the absence to meet multiple or all requirements of a clause
- The company documents how it will address these non-conformances and forwards these documents to the RCB for approval

5. Certification Audit (stage 2)

- The Certification Audit is an objective assessment of the organizational procedures and practices that will be conducted against the documented management system
- The auditor will interview staff and look for records (evidence) that the management system is operated in line with the documented management system
- Findings of the audit will be presented in a written report
- Non-conformances will be fed into the CAP
- Upon a successful certification audit and the decision to grant certification, a certificate of registration is awarded; note that the audit team of the RCB can only recommend

---

4 Note that officially only the outcome of a Certification Audit can result into nonconformities. Deficiencies determined during the Initial Audit are therefore in essence potential nonconformities at the time the Certification Audit is conducted.

certification. It is the certification board of the RCB who decides whether or not certification is awarded after reviewing the technical review of the audit report

- The organization is allowed to use the RCB's certification mark and the relevant ISO/IEC 20000 certification mark for three years; this mark cannot be used on products

6. Surveillance Audits

- A program of surveillance audits is arranged to verify that the ISO/IEC 20000 requirements continue to be met
- Non-conformances during this program go into the CAP
- Surveillance audits are conducted over a three-year cycle
- They are usually conducted every six to twelve months
- Any outstanding CAPs are audited during these audits, as well as areas the auditors deem necessary to be assessed again. For example, when a service provider has undergone a merger, the surveillance audit should focus on the affected areas.

7. Re-certification Audits

- Every three years a re-certification audit is conducted
- The audit is similar to the Certification Audit but it will take less time, unless the scope of certification has changed
- In the event the certificate cannot be awarded, identified non-conformances must be corrected and another audit must be performed to have the certificate awarded again
- Upon re-certification the surveillance audits will start over again over a period of three years

4.5   Scoping and applicability

Applicability means the relevance to the organization's business.

The applicability of ISO/IEC 20000 is broad and can be applied to internal and external service providers (ISPs and ESPs), large, small, commercial and non-commercial organizations.

The service provider's entire organization or part of it can be certified. The latter is more common. All ISO/IEC 20000 processes need to be in place and be controlled by the service provider even in the event the processes are operated by other parties. More information about eligibility and scoping can be found in the ISO/IEC 20000-3 document.

The Scope of Certification defines the effective range of the Management System. A Scoping Statement includes:
- The services encompassed by the audit
- Geographical and local boundaries
- Organizational and functional boundaries
- Technical boundaries

The figure below shows a simplified example of boundaries within the scope of certification.

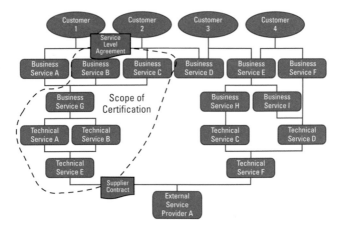

Figure 4.2 Boundaries within scope of certification

The preferred style of the scoping statement is shown in Table 4.2 below.

Table 4.2 Preferred style of scoping statement

The Service Management System of
<Name of service provider organizational unit>
that delivers <Service(s)> to
<Customer organizational name and/or name of organizational unit>
from <Geographical location>.

5 Relationships to frameworks

This chapter describes ISO/IEC 20000's relation to ITIL® and Risk Management. Note that the standard also relates to other frameworks.

5.1 Relationship to ITIL®

The experienced IT Infrastructure Library (ITIL) enthusiast will easily recognize similarities between portions of the ISO/IEC 20000 standard and ITIL's best practices. However, there are areas in the standard where ITIL is not the first choice when looking for guidance. Examples are strategic risk management, IT governance, and project or program management.

The main difference remains that ISO/IEC 20000 is a global ITSM standard which prescribes the minimal requirements for effective ITSM. And ITIL describes industry best practices for ITSM that are worthwhile considering.

Applying IT Infrastructure Library best practices will assist a service provider in achieving the quality of Service Management required by ISO/IEC 20000. The relationship between the processes of the ISO/IEC 20000, the 2005 and the 2011 version, and the ITIL processes is illustrated in the table below.

Table 6.1 Cross-reference between processes in ISO/IEC 20000:2011, ISO/IEC 2000:2005 and ITIL, edition 2011

Main Processes in ISO/IEC 20000:2011[1]	Processes in ISO/IEC 20000:2005	Processes in ITIL, edition 2011
Design and Transition of New or Changed Services	Planning and Implementing new or Changed Services	No immediate process equivalent
Service Level Management	Service Level Management	Service Level Management
Service Reporting	Service Reporting	Service Reporting[2]
Service Continuity and Availability Management	Service Continuity and Availability Management	IT Service Continuity Management Availability Management
Budgeting and Accounting for Services	Budgeting and Accounting for IT Services	Financial Management for IT Services
Capacity Management	Capacity Management	Capacity Management
Information Security Management	Information Security Management	Information Security Management
Business Relationship Management	Business Relationship Management	Business Relationship Management
Supplier Management	Supplier Management	Supplier Management
Incident and Service Request Management	Incident Management	Incident Management Request Fulfilment
Problem Management	Problem Management	Problem Management
Configuration Management	Configuration Management	Service Asset and Configuration Management
Change Management	Change Management	Change Management
Release and Deployment Management	Release Management	Release and Deployment Management

1 Note that the standard does not specifically require a *process* in some cases. Examples are Service Reporting and Capacity Management even though both are positioned in the Service Delivery set of *processes*.
2 Note that Service Reporting is considered a Method and Technique in ITIL Edition 2011

From a naming perspective, the following ITIL processes have no immediate equivalent in ISO/IEC 20000. However, some of the ISO/IEC 20000 processes do address portions of ITIL processes that have been given a different name. The second column in the table below makes note of such partial relationships.

Table 6.2 Partial relationships between ISO/IEC 20000 and ITIL

Processes in ITIL, edition 2011, with no direct equivalent process in ISO/IEC 20000	Processes in ISO/IEC 20000:2011 which address (portions of) this ITIL Process
Strategy Management for IT Services	Service Management System (limited) Design and Transition of New or Changed Services (limited)
Service Portfolio Management	Design and Transition of New or Changed Services (limited)
Charging (as part of Financial Management for IT Services)	Not applicable
Demand Management	Capacity Management
Design Coordination	Service Management System (limited) Design and Transition of New or Changed Services
Service Catalog Management	Service Level Management
Transition Planning and Support	Service Management System (limited) Design and Transition of New or Changed Services
Service Asset Management	Configuration Management
Service Validation and Testing	Release and Deployment Management Design and Transition of New or Changed Services
Change Evaluation	Change Management Design and Transition of New or Changed Services

Processes in ITIL, edition 2011, with no direct equivalent process in ISO/IEC 20000	Processes in ISO/IEC 20000:2011 which address (portions of) this ITIL Process
Event Management	Incident and Service Request Management
Access Management	Service Continuity and Availability Management Information Security Management
The Seven-Step Improvement Process	Plan the SMS (Plan) Implement and Operate the SMS (Do) Monitor and Review the SMS (Check) Maintain and Improve the SMS (Act)

5.2 Relationship to risk management

As stated in Chapter 2, ISO/IEC 20000's section 4 "Service Management System general requirements" includes requirements involving strategic risk management[3]. The service provider is required to ensure that risks to services are assessed, managed and reviewed. Furthermore, the service provider is required to determine an approach to accept risks and set targets for the improvements in risk reduction. Given the challenges organizations are faced with in meeting this requirement, often due to the lack of having a strategic risk management framework and/or process in place, some guidance is provided in this chapter.

Risks may affect the achievement of an organization's objectives, including those of the service provider. The scope of risks can be

---

3 Note that strategic risk management covers much more than those risks that are to be managed by Information Security Management process and the Service Continuity and Availability Management process. Strategic risk management's scope is much broader. More information will be described in this chapter.

strategic, tactical, and operational. The scope can also include process risks and project risks.

Risks can impact:
- Environmental, technological, safety and security outcomes
- Commercial, financial and economic measures, and
- Social, cultural, political and reputation aspects

All activities of an organization involve risks and should be managed, including Service Management activities.

Risk Management aids decision making by taking account of uncertainty and the possibility of future events or circumstances (intended or unintended) and their effects on agreed objectives. Risk Management includes the application of logical and systematic methods for:
- Communicating and consulting throughout the risk management process;
- Establishing the context for identifying, analyzing, evaluating, treating risk associated with any activity, process, function or product;
- Monitoring and reviewing risks;
- Reporting and recording the results appropriately

Risk Assessment is that part of Risk Management which provides a structured process that identifies how objectives may be affected, and analyzes the risk in term of consequences and their probabilities before deciding on whether further treatment is required.

Risk Assessment attempts to answer the following fundamental questions:

- What can happen and why (by Risk Identification)?
- What are the consequences?
- What is the probability of their future occurrence?
- Are there any factors that mitigate the consequence of the risk or that reduce the probability of the risk?

A **Risk Management Framework** provides the policies, procedures and organizational arrangements that will embed Risk Management throughout the organization at all levels.

An organization should have a policy or strategy for deciding when and how risks should be assessed. When carrying out Risk Assessments the following should be clear:

- The context and objectives of the organization,
- The extent and type of risks that are tolerable and how unacceptable risks are to be treated,
- How Risk Assessment integrates into organizational processes,
- Methods and techniques to be used for Risk Assessment, and their contribution to the Risk Management process,
- Accountability, responsibility and authority for performing risk assessment,
- Resources available to carry out Risk Assessment,
- How the Risk Assessment will be reported and reviewed.

Figure 6.1 below shows ISO 31000's risk management framework.

The **Risk Management process** should be

- An integral part of management (including Service Management),

Figure 6.1 ISO 31000 risk management framework

- Embedded in the culture and practices of the service provider's organization, and
- Tailored to the business and IT processes of the organization

Critical Success Factors of the Risk Management process are:
- Active Leadership Commitment
- Quality Communication
- Clear and Concise Context
- Process Culture
- Continual Improvement Mentality

Figure 6.2 below shows ISO 31000's risk management process.

As referenced already, the international ISO standard for risk management is ISO 31000. The supporting ISO/IEC 31010 document provides additional guidance on the standard's risk management framework and a risk management process.

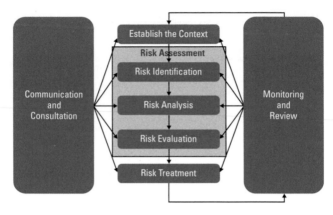

Figure 6.2 ISO 31000 risk management process

There are several additional risk management approaches
available which can support the efforts of determining and
managing the strategic risks to ITSM. What most of these
approaches have in common is to first analyze the potential
risks, then assess each risk on probability and impact and finally
determine the risk mitigations and the management of each.
Examples of risk management frameworks are Management of
Risks (M_o_R) and the UK's HM Treasury Orange Book.

6 Alignment with other standards

This chapter explains ISO/IEC 20000's alignment with ISO 9001 and ISO/IEC 27001.

6.1 Alignment with ISO 9001

The 2011 version of ISO/IEC 20000 has undergone some enhancements to better align with the ISO 9000 standard for Quality Management, as mentioned in Appendix B.

The table below shows at a high level how both the ISO 9001 and the ISO/IEC 20000 standard align.

Table 6.4 Alignment with ISO 9001

ISO 9001:2008 Section: 4. Quality management system	Alignment with ISO/IEC 20000-1:2011 Section:
4 Quality management system 4.1 General requirements	4.5 Establish and improve the SMS (Plan-Do-Check-Act)
4.2 Documentation requirements	4.3 Document management

ISO 9001:2008 Section: 5. Management responsibilities	Alignment with ISO/IEC 20000-1:2011 Section:
5.1 Management commitment	4.1.1 Management commitment
5.2 Customer focus	4.1.4 Management representative
5.3 Quality policy	4.4.1 Provision of resources 4.1.2 Service management policy
5.4 Planning	4.5.2 Plan the SMS
5.5 Responsibility, authority and communication	4.1.1 Management commitment 4.1.3 Authority, responsibility and communication 4.1.4 Management representative
5.6 Management review	4.5.4.3 Management review

ISO 9001:2008 Section: 6. Resource management	Alignment with ISO/IEC 20000-1:2011 Section:
6.1 Provision of resources	**4.4.1** Provision of resources
6.2 Human resources	**4.4.2** Human resources
6.3 Infrastructure	-- (Partially in 4.4.1 Provision of resources)
6.4 Work environment	--

ISO 9001:2008 Section: 7. Product realization	Alignment with ISO/IEC 20000-1:2011 Section:
7.1 Planning of product realization	**4.5.2** Plan the SMS
7.2 Customer-related processes	**5.2** Plan new or changed services
7.3 Design and development	**5.3** Design and development of new or changed services
7.4 Purchasing	**4.2** Governance of processes operated by other parties **7.2** Supplier Management
7.5 Production and service provision	**4.5.3** Implement and operate the SMS **9.1** Configuration Management

ISO 9001:2008 Section: 8. Measurement, analyses and improvement	Alignment with ISO/IEC 20000-1:2011 Section:
8.1 General	**4.5.4** Monitor and review the SMS **4.5.4.1** General
8.2 Monitoring and measurement	**6.2** Service Reporting **4.5.4.2** Internal Audit **4.5.4.3** Management review
8.4 Analysis of data	**6.2** Service Reporting
8.5 Improvement	**4.5.5** Maintain and improve the SMS

6.2   Alignment with ISO/IEC 27001

The 2011 edition of ISO/IEC 20000 has undergone some enhancements to better align in particular with the ISO/IEC 27001 standard for Information Security Management.

As mentioned in Chapter 5, the requirements of the ISO/
IEC 20000 management system have been enhanced to better
synchronize with the one of the ISO/IEC 27001 standard.

The table below shows at a high level how both the ISO/IEC
27001 and the Information Security Management process of the
ISO/IEC 20000 standard align (Table 6.5).

In the two columns on the left the Information Security
Management requirements according to ISO/IEC 20000 are
listed. The two columns on the right show the corresponding
ISO/IEC 27001 requirements.

In ISO/IEC 27002 Code of Practice for Information Security
Management, more guidance can be found to implement and
meet the Information Security Management requirements.
Whenever an ISO/IEC 27001 clause number is referenced
beginning with "A", (e.g. A.5.1.1) there is a corresponding control
in the ISO/IEC 27002 document with the same number (e.g. 5.1.1)
with additional helpful information to meet the respective
requirement.

Table 6.6 Alignment with ISO/IEC 27001

ISO/IEC 20000:2011		ISO/IEC 27001:2005	
Clause number	Clause	Clause number	Clause
6.6	**Information Security Management**		
6.6.1	**Information security policy**		
	Management with appropriate authority shall approve an information security policy taking	A.5.1.1	Information security policy

ISO/IEC 20000:2011		ISO/IEC 27001:2005	
	into consideration the service requirements, statutory and regulatory requirements and contractual obligations.		
	Management shall:		
	a) communicate the information security policy and the importance of conforming to the policy to appropriate personnel within the service provider, customer and suppliers;	5.1	Management commitment
	b) ensure that information security management objectives are established;	5.1	Management commitment
	c) define the approach to be taken for the management of information security risks and the criteria for accepting risks;	4.2.1, 5.1	Establish the ISMS, Management commitment
	d) ensure that information security risk assessments are conducted at planned intervals;	4.2.3	Monitor and review the ISMS
	e) ensure that internal information security audits are conducted;	5.1	Management commitment
	f) ensure that audit results are reviewed to identify opportunities for improvement.	6	Internal ISMS audits

ISO/IEC 20000:2011		ISO/IEC 27001:2005	
6.6.2	**Information security controls**		
	The service provider shall implement and operate physical, administrative and technical information security controls in order to:		
	a) preserve confidentiality, integrity and accessibility of information assets;	A.6.1.5, A.6.2.1, A.6.2.2, A.6.2.3, A.7.2.1, A.9.2.4, A.11, A.10.4, A.10.5, A.10.6.1, A.10.8.1, A.10.8.5, A.10.9.1, A.10.9.3, A.12.2.1, A.12.2.2, A.12.3, A.12.5, A.13.2.1, A.13.2.3, A.14.1.3, A.15.1.6	Confidentiality Agreements controls, Identification of risks related to external parties controls, Addressing security when dealing with customers controls, Addressing security in third party agreements controls, Classification guidelines controls, Equipment maintenance controls, Protection against malicious and mobile code controls, Access control, Back-up controls, Network controls, Information exchange policies and procedures controls, Business information systems controls, Electronic commerce controls, Publicly available information controls, Input data validation controls, Control of internal processing,

ISO/IEC 20000:2011		ISO/IEC 27001:2005	
			Cryptographic controls, Security in development and support processes controls, Responsibilities and procedures controls, Collection of evidence controls, Developing and implementing continuity plans including information security controls, Regulation of cryptographic controls,
	b) fulfill the requirements of the information security policy;	A.5	Security policy controls
	c) achieve information security management objectives;	A.5	Security policy controls
	d) manage risks related to information security.	A.5.1.1, A.6.1.2, A.7.1.1, A.14.1.1	Information security policy document controls, Information security co-ordination controls; Inventory of assets controls; Including information security in the business continuity management process controls
	These information security controls shall be documented and shall describe the risks to which the controls relate their operation and maintenance.	A.5.1.1, A.6.1.3, A.7.1.1, A.7.1.3, A.8.1.1, A.8.3.2, A.9.2.3, A.10.1.1, A.10.3.2,	Information security policy document controls, Allocation of information security responsibilities controls, Inventory of assets controls, Acceptable use of assets controls, Roles and responsibilities controls,

ISO/IEC 20000:2011		ISO/IEC 27001:2005	
		A.10.5.1, A.10.7.1, A.10.7.4, A.10.9.1, A.11.1.1, A.12.2.2, A.12.5.1, A.12.5.3, A.13.2.1, A.14.1.3, A.15.1.1, A.15.2.2, A.15.2.1	Return of assets controls, Cabling security controls, Documented operating procedures, System acceptance controls, Information back-up controls, Management of removable media controls, Security of system documentation controls, Electronic commerce controls, Access control policy controls, Control of internal processing controls, Change control procedures, Restrictions on changes to software packages controls, Responsibilities and procedures controls, Developing and implementing continuity plans including information security controls, Identification of applicable legislation controls, Technical compliance checking controls, Information systems audit controls,
	The service provider shall review the effectiveness of information security controls.	4.2.2, 4.2.3	Implement and operate the ISMS, Monitor and review the ISMS

ISO/IEC 20000:2011		ISO/IEC 27001:2005	
	The service provider shall take necessary actions and report on the actions taken.	**4.2.4**	Maintain and improve the ISMS
	The service provider shall identify external organizations that have a need to access, use or manage the service provider's information or services.	**A.6.2**	External parties controls
	The service provider shall document, agree and implement information security controls with these external organizations.	**A.10.8**	Exchange of information controls
6.6.3	**Information security changes and incidents**		
	Requests for change shall be assessed to identify:	**A.5.1.2, A.8.3.3, A.10.1.2, A.10.2.3, A.12.5**	Review of the information security policy controls, Removal of access rights controls, Change Management controls, Managing changes to third party services controls, Security in development and support processes controls,
	a) new or changed information security risks;		
	b) potential impact on the existing information security policy and controls.		

ISO/IEC 20000:2011		ISO/IEC 27001:2005	
	Information security incidents shall be managed using the incident management procedures, with a priority appropriate to the information security risks.	**4.2.2,** **4.2.3,** **4.3.3,** **A.13**	Implement and operate the ISMS, Monitor and review the ISMS, Control of records, Information security incident management controls,
	The service provider shall analyze the types, volumes and impacts of information security incidents.	**A.13**	Information security incident management controls
	Information security incidents shall be reported and reviewed to identify opportunities for improvement.	**4.2.3,** **A.13**	Monitor and review the ISMS, Information security incident management controls,

7 ISO/IEC 20000 and communication

The ISO/IEC 20000-1:2011 standard has 15 requirements for the service provider to communicate. This does not include the requirements implying that the service provider should communicate when referring to required activities such as report, review, evaluate, establish awareness, obtain feedback and obtain status information. Neither does this include the process integration requirements, ensuring communication within the service provider's organization. Solid communication can therefore certainly be considered a key to effective management of IT Services.

While on the business-side an organization may find functions responsible for (market or media) communication, within IT organizations one rarely finds a Communications Director for example. Traditionally, the service provider's (executive) management is expected to cover the necessary (strategic) communication. And when (tactical or operational) communication needs improvement it is left to a line manager or the Human Resource department to identify room for improvement areas.

Service providers attempting to become more process-oriented, more service-oriented and more customer-focused are the first to experience how the lack of communication is hindering their efforts in accomplishing these transformations. Customers assume that IT services are managed end-to-end, which requires processes to be implemented and managed across the board supported by cross-functional technology platforms. Taking this into account it is not a surprise that close to 25 percent of the ISO/IEC 20000 requirements refer to communication-related aspects, again not including the process integration requirements.

Communication is a two-way stream endeavor. The sender of a message is involved and the receiver of this message is involved. The sender transmits the intended message and the receiver transmits the feedback message, allowing the sender to verify his/her intended message. On paper this makes sense; however, in reality the feedback message does not always receive the appropriate amount of attention. For example, procedures are developed without the appropriate level of involvement of those who are supposed to follow them.

One of the reasons for insufficient attention to feedback is the choice of media we use to communicate. The diagram[1] below shows how the feedback loop can improve by choosing the right medium and stimulus[2] (Figure 7.1).

When taking into account that adopting ITSM best practices comes along with the management of organizational change, the vehicle you choose to communicate is crucial and requires thorough consideration. It is particularly important when appropriately responding to and managing the resistance to change.

On the transmitting side, open communication will contribute to successful communication. Choosing the right media is just

1 Adapted from Hellriegel and Slocum, Organizational Behavior, Southwestern 2007
2 A stimulus is something that incites to action or exertion or quickens action, feeling, thought, feedback, etc.

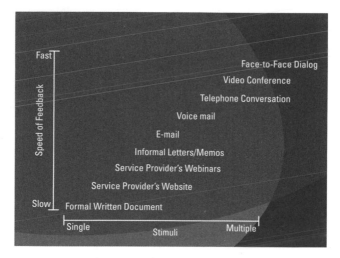

Figure 7.1 Improving the communications feedback loop

one element of open communication. Communication that builds trust, has no hidden agendas, and reveals intended goals are additional elements characterizing open communication. For example, ISO/IEC 20000 states that management is required to ensure that its personnel are aware of how they contribute to the achievement of Service Management objectives and the fulfillment of service requirements. By setting clear expectations and measurable targets, trust can be built and intended goals can be achieved.

On the receiving end, constructive feedback will contribute to successful communication. Corrective feedback, positive feedback from management and from peers and internal feedback are elements that are part of constructive feedback. Also, active listening is a technique that is highly recommended to improve communication. It involves paying attention, withholding judgment, reflecting, clarifying, summarizing, and sharing. With well over 30 requirements mentioning the word "review", the ISO/IEC 20000 standard constantly requires the service provider to seek feedback and act upon it accordingly.

When keeping all of the above in mind - the identification, documenting, management, review and improvement of all the communication - the standard requires an easy-to-use Communication Plan. This could be a useful instrument that contributes to successful communication. A template of such a plan is displayed below (Table 7.1).

Although the standard does not specifically require having a Communication Plan, it does require a communication procedure in section 4.1.3b) "Authority, responsibility and communication", which could include such plan. A Communication Plan is useful for effectively organizing and managing the service provider's communications.

Table 7.1 Template for a Communication Plan

Audience	Communication Contents	Frequency	Medium	Data Source	Delivered by	Date Delivered	Expected Result
Service provider Staff	Management shall communicate the scope, policy and objectives for Service Management	Quarterly	Town hall meeting	ITSM Dashboard	CIO	January, April, July, October	Awareness, Commitment, Setting of Direction and Expectations
Service provider Staff	Management shall communicate the importance of fulfilling service requirements	Monthly	Team meetings	Service Level Reports	Line Managers	Every month	Service Quality focused Staff Members
Etc.							

ISO/IEC 20000:2011 – A Pocket Guide

8 ISO/IEC 20000-1:2011

In this chapter the ISO/IEC 20000-1:2011 is referenced and described in a way that allows for easy interpretation of the requirements. This chapter does not provide a copy of the ISO/IEC 20000-1:2011 standard. Not all requirements are referenced.

8.1 Management in general

Using ISO/IEC 20000 requires a well-balanced approach using management techniques, policies, plans, delegation, effective communication, cultivation of the best people, sharing of knowledge and other management instruments. This is implied with the system approach to management principle of Quality Management on which ISO/IEC 20000 is based on.

8.2 Scope – clause 1 of ISO/IEC 20000-1

In today's business the need to demonstrate the ability to provide services that meet customer requirements is evident. This can be achieved by standardization of the Service Management System (SMS). The requirements as applied in ISO/IEC 20000 represent an industry consensus on quality standards for the SMS.

It can be used by service providers to:
- Monitor and improve their service quality
- Benchmark or baseline their SMS
- Serve as the basis for an independent assessment or audit which may lead to formal certification
- Demonstrate the ability to provide services that meet customer requirements

It can be used by the customers of IT services to:

- Assure a consistent service delivery approach by all its service providers
- Support their due diligence efforts when selecting a service provider
- Provide understanding of what to expect from a service provider

Service delivery is defined in a number of closely related management techniques and Service Management processes organized in a SMS. The service provider's SMS turns service requirements and expectations of customers into services satisfying the customer's objectives (Figure 8.1).

Figure 8.1 Service Management System positioning

Considering the variety of specific business needs, a service provider may decide that additional objectives and controls are necessary, in particular when referring to the service provider's needs.

The SMS components are referenced in the subsequent sections.

8.3   Application – clause 1.2 of ISO/IEC 20000-1

The ISO/IEC 20000 requirements apply to all service providers, independent of industry, whether operating in a commercial environment, not-for-profit, or government environment, the size of the service provider's organization, or where the services are delivered.

Complying with the standard's requirements can be achieved by providing evidence. Evidence manifests itself in the form of documents and records. Documents express the service provider's intentions. Records provide proof that the service provider is indeed doing what the service provider intended to do.

The vast majority of the evidence to be provided revolves around the governance of service requirements and the management of these requirements from obtaining them, translating them into services and meeting those service requirements through the delivery of the services. The management aspects and the work involved are organized in the SMS. This is why the SMS consists of management areas with management requirements to be met and it consists of processes addressing the work involved with process requirements to be met. When meeting these requirements of the standard, the service provider's quality of service is more robust compared to a service provider not meeting the standard's requirements.

The management requirements are described in section 4 of the standard:
4. Service management system general requirements.

The process requirements are described in sections 5 through 9 of the standard:
5. Design and transition of new or changed services
6. Service delivery processes
7. Relationship processes
8. Resolution processes
9. Control processes

The paragraphs below describe each section of the ISO/IEC 20000:2011 standard in greater detail. It is not intended to reference the identical text of the standard. The standard's requirements are paraphrased in the author's own words to enhance the interpretation of the each requirement. The number in brackets references the standard's section number.

8.4 (4) Service management system general requirements

(4.1) Management responsibility

(4.1.1) Management commitment

Through various ways, the service provider's executive management is required to provide evidence of its intentions and accomplishments regarding the SMS. The standard seeks proof of active commitment by executive management. Since communication is an important responsibility of executive management, many requirements look for evidence about communication aspects. Executive management is required to communicate to the interested parties:

1. The scope of Service Management, the Service Management policy and the objectives to be met with Service Management
2. Why it is important to the customer and to the service provider to meet the service requirements, combined with meeting legal and regulatory requirements

In addition, executive management is required to:

1. Ensure there is a Service Management Plan (more about this plan is in section 4.5.2 of the standard), make sure that the plan is implemented and maintained in line with the policies, objectives and requirements

2. Ensure there are sufficient resources available such as funding, time, people, tools, facilities, etc. to meet these policies, objectives and requirements
3. Ensure that organizational risks that can negatively impact the policies, objectives and requirements are continuously analyzed, assessed and managed. (More guidance on organizational risk management can be found in Chapter 6)
4. Look for ways to continuously improve the SMS

(4.1.2) Service management policy

It is the responsibility of the service provider's executive management to create, implement, maintain and continuously improve the Service Management policy. The standard is very specific about what the policy needs to address. For example, the policy needs to:

1. Apply to the service provider's Service Management objectives and describe an approach to meeting and reviewing these objectives
2. Express the service provider's commitments to meeting the customer's service requirements and to continually seek for ways to improve the SMS

In addition, executive management is required to:
1. Communicate the policy to all the stakeholders involved
2. Frequently review it to ensure the policy still applies to the Service Management objectives and service requirements

(4.1.3) Authority, responsibility and communication

The success of meeting the Service Management objectives highly depends on the service provider's executive management and personnel. It is particularly important when considering the three topics of this section of the standard: authority, responsibility and communication. Given the latter topic's magnitude we decided to provide more guidance on communication in Chapter 7.

A typical challenge for service providers is to assign the often new roles of (for example) the Service Owner(s), Process Owner(s) and Process Manager(s). A Service Owner is responsible to manage a service end-to-end throughout its entire lifecycle. Ideally, Service Owners "reside" high in the service provider's organizational chart to ensure a sufficient level of authority. Figure 8.2 below displays a typical way of positioning Process Owners and Process Managers in an organizational chart. Process Owners are accountable for the process. Process Managers are responsible and therefore more involved with establishing the process and implementing the supporting procedures. Process Operatives do the work and operate on a Work Instruction level.

IT Departments vs. Processes

Service Mgmt	Application Mgmt	Database Mgmt	Server Mgmt	Network Mgmt

Change Management Process

Process Owner	Process Manager	Process Manager	Process Manager	Process Manager
	Process Operatives	Process Operatives	Process Operatives	Process Operatives

Figure 8.2 Organizational chart showing Process Owners and Process Managers

Finding the right people to take on these, often new, roles is the
first hurdle. Then the question arises of which responsibilities
need to be assigned to these roles. ITSM best practices
frameworks provide textbook answers to this question. However,
assigning responsibilities to a Process Owner, for example, may
require a shift in responsibilities. Backing up these new roles (and
responsibilities) with the appropriate authority levels is crucial
for the success of these roles. Authority can be granted directly
to the person involved, or indirectly through the manager of the
(new) Service Owner or Process Owner.

Given the criticality of these topics, it is to be expected that the
standard has several requirements addressing this often delicate
matter. It is the responsibility of executive management to:
1. Define and maintain these Service Management authorities
   and responsibilities
2. Document, define and deploy procedure(s) relating to
   communication

(4.1.4) Management representative
One of the critical success factors for meeting the Service
Management objectives, adhering to the Service Management
policies and meeting the customer requirements is the active
backing of executive management. The standard is very specific
about this and even requires that a member of the executive
management team with the right authorities is solely responsible
for this success.

The standard continues with listing the responsibilities of this executive management team member such as:

1. Ensure the Service Management objectives and service requirements are being met and that the Service Management policy is being adhered to
2. Ensure that roles, responsibilities and authorities are assigned appropriately
3. Ensure that the Service Management processes are integrated with each other and align with SMS areas such as Service Management policies and plans, and support Service Management objectives, service requirements and legal and statutory requirements
4. Ensure to communicate with the rest of the executive management team members about the success rate of the SMS and the services and how to continuously improve those

(4.2) Governance of processes operated by other parties

The IT industry is becoming more and more specialized. This has resulted in more frequent "build or buy" or sourcing discussions than ever before in the relatively short history of IT. As a result, the dependency on (specialized) third parties has increased and probably will continue to do so. Consequently, certain processes, or parts of processes, contributing to the delivery and support of services, are often executed outside the immediate boundaries of control of the service provider. While this might be the case, the standard is very clear that it is the service provider's responsibility to determine those (parts of the) processes and still show how the service provider is governing it all.

For example, the service provider needs to show evidence of:
1. Accountability for the (parts of the) processes

2. Authority and control over the (parts of the) processes to
    ensure the standard's process requirements are being met, that
    process performance is being measured and that the (parts of
    the) processes are continuously improved

Note that when the standard refers to "other parties" these
parties could be a third party, but could also be an in-house
party that executes a (portion of a) process. Third parties are
managed through Supplier Management (with the help of a
Supplier Contract) and in-house parties through Service Level
Management (with the help of a documented agreement).

(4.3) Documentation management

(4.3.1) Establish and maintain documents
Documents are a crucial part of providing the necessary evidence
proving compliance with the requirements of the ISO/IEC 20000
standards. Documentation is also a management instrument to
ensure the service provider's organization's data, information and
knowledge are accessible and shared when needed. Documents
and records contribute to the success of the SMS. For example:
1. Customer requirements are captured and agreed
2. Services are designed, developed, deployed, maintained
    and improved through a series of documented steps, each
    generating documented deliverables to enable the control
    and the continuous synchronization with these customer
    requirements

The standard lists a number of examples of documents in support
of the activities as mentioned above including policies, plans,
documented processes and procedures, a Service Catalog, SLAs,
etc.

(4.3.2) Control of documents

As mentioned in chapter 4.3 of this book, documents are evidence of the service provider's intentions.

This section of the standard is closely aligned with the corresponding section in the ISO 9001 standard about Document Management. It requires a Document Management control procedure – that is, a procedure covering the document lifecycle, including the roles and responsibilities involved.

The document controls required by the standard address the typical steps in the lifecycle of a document - for example, the creation of a document, the approval of a document, the review and maintenance of a document and the distribution of a document.

Other controls address document management controls such as versioning control, status control and the protection of documents.

(4.3.3) Control of records

Records also serve as necessary proof that the service provider is indeed following through on its documented intentions. Examples of records are meeting minutes, up-to-date action items, Incident records, Problem records, Change records, log files, etc.

Records also need to be managed through a procedure. The procedure needs to describe steps addressing the identification, storage, retrieval, retention, protection and disposal of records.

(4.4) Resource management

(4.4.1) Provision of resources

As mentioned in section 4.1 of the standard, the service provider's executive management's intentions require active commitment. One way of proving such commitment is by making the necessary resources available to create, implement, maintain and continuously improve the SMS. These resources should be dedicated to continuously measure the customer's satisfaction and needs so as to always meet the service requirements.

The standard spells out the resources it is referring to:
1. Human resources (e.g. the service provider's executive management and personnel, third party personnel)
2. Technical resources (e.g. tools and technology supporting the service provider's processes and personnel)
3. Information resources (e.g. documents and records needed for the provisioning of services as required by the customer)
4. Financial resources (e.g. budgets and allocation of funds to enable the SMS and its intended outcomes)

(4.4.2) Human resources

The human resources are given special attention by the standard. The service provider is required by ISO/IEC 20000 to have competent personnel involved with meeting the service requirements. Depending on the needs of the customer and the services to be provided to meet those needs, specific roles and responsibilities are to be assigned the service provider's personnel, or to the personnel of other parties as appropriate.

Each role and responsibility requires a certain skill set, a level of experience and expertise. When a gap is identified in the service

provider's personnel's skill set, experience and expertise, the
service provider has two options: either bridge this gap through
(formal) training and education, or find it externally through
hiring or sourcing.

The standard requires that the service provider continuously
identifies the necessary competencies and (potential) gaps
and evaluates the actions taken to meet the required levels of
competencies.

Another component of this section of the standard addresses the
need for the service provider to make its personnel continuously
aware of their contribution to the success of the SMS.

(4.5) Establish and improve the SMS

(4.5.1) Define scope

As mentioned chapter 4.5 of this book, it rarely happens that
a service provider obtains ISO/IEC 20000 certification for all
its services. By limiting the scope, certification can be reached
faster. Another reason for limiting the scope is to only include the
critical services within the scope of certification. Along the same
lines of reasoning, service providers in commercial environments
wisely choose their scope of certification. Customers of services
provided that are not part of the scope may get the wrong
impression. The scope definition can help or hinder the service
provider. Especially with the industry becoming more educated
on ISO/IEC 20000, simply stating that the company is ISO/IEC
20000 certified will most likely lead to having to answer a follow
up question enquiring about the scope of certification.

ISO/IEC TR 20000-3 provides guidance of the scope definition and applicability of the standard. service providers seeking certification are recommended to obtain a copy of this document.

Besides determining which services are within the scope of certification, there are requirements such as the geographical location(s) of the service provider and the customer(s), ownership and technology used to support the services and the fact that certification can only be granted to one legal entity.

(4.5.2) Plan the SMS (Plan)

Just like ISO 9001 and the ISO/IEC 27001 standard, ISO/IEC 20000 also refers to Deming's Quality Circle (PDCA: Plan-Do-Check-Act) to plan, implement and operate, monitor and review and maintain and improve the SMS (Figure 8.3). Service providers are free to choose another quality improvement approach, model, or process if so desired. Given the generic nature of Deming's Quality Circle it will not take too much effort to map the requirements of the standard to the quality improvement framework of your choice.

The PDCA model assumes that to provide appropriate quality, the following steps must be undertaken repeatedly:

- Plan - establish the objectives, service requirements and processes necessary to deliver the required results as well as the resources, frameworks, approaches needed in support of this. This stage is completed with agreements that are measurable and realistic, and a Service Management plan of how they are to be achieved.
- Do – implement and operate the SMS. Services are now designed, deployed, maintained and improved according to the Service Management plan.

Continuous Service Quality Control and Consolidation

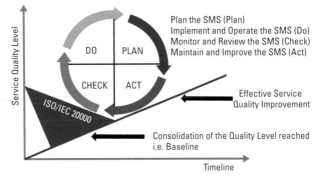

Figure 8.3 Plan-Do-Check-Act model for continuous service quality control and consolidation (Deming's Quality Circle)

- Check - monitor and measure processes and services against policies, objectives and requirements. This stage includes audits and management reviews.
- Act - identify actions to continuously improve the performance of the SMS and the services.

By repeating this cycle, a step-by-step quality improvement can be assured. This is known as the 'uphill cycle of never-ending improvement'.

Documentation is very important in successful application of the PDCA model. As the output of each activity is the input of the next activity in the model, a constant feedback is realized and transparency in relationships between processes is created.

The Service Management plan is an important document created during the Plan phase of the SMS. The standard has specific

requirements for the topics to be addressed in the plan. Examples
of these required items are:

1. The service provider's objectives
2. The service requirements to meet the needs of the customers
3. References to policies (e.g. Service Management policy),
    standards and legal and statutory requirements to be
    adhered to
4. References to process-specific plans
5. The roles, responsibilities and authorities defined and
    assigned to the service provider's personnel
6. The resources that are needed to accomplish a successful SMS
7. The way the SMS works together - for example, with the
    processes of other parties
8. The way the service provider analyzes, assesses and manages
    organizational risks which may affect the success of the SMS
9. The way the effectiveness of the SMS and the services will be
    monitored, reviewed and continuously improved

(4.5.3) Implement and operate the SMS (Do)

During this phase of the service quality improvement cycle the
service provider designs, builds, deploys, maintains and improves
the SMS and the service as intended in the Service Management
plan. Now:

1. Funds are allocated
2. Roles, responsibilities and authorities are assigned
3. Resources are managed
4. Organizational risks are analyzed, assessed and managed
5. Service management processes are designed, implemented
    and managed
6. The performance of the SMS and the services are monitored
    and reported on

(4.5.4) Monitor and review the SMS (Check)

(4.5.4.1) General

The service provider has to determine how to monitor and measure the performance of the SMS and the services. Internal audits and management reviews are required methods that will contribute to meeting the requirements of this section of the standard.

(4.5.4.2) Internal audits

Those service providers whose organization has an established internal auditing department should consider involving these colleagues in support of meeting the internal auditing requirements of the standard. A word of caution is needed though, as your internal auditing department may not have a background in Service Management. This gap can be bridged in most cases through formal training and education.

Service providers who prefer not to involve their internal audit department or have no such department can consider using a trusted consulting firm to assist with meeting these requirements.

Internal audits have to be planned and executed regularly. Once certification has been obtained, the outcomes of these internal audits provide a barometer of the service provider's continuous adherence to the standard's requirements. The internal audits could be planned before a (re-)certification audit, in between surveillance audits, after a major (organizational) change, etc.

Documents and records need to provide the necessary evidence such as:
• An audit plan

- An audit procedure
- Audit roles and responsibilities
- Audit reports with audit results and communication records of the findings
- Action items as a follow up to the audit results with status updates

Note that ISO 19011 provides guidance on auditing a management system.

(4.5.4.3) Management review
The service provider's executive management is required to review the performance of the SMS and the services frequently and decide on whether or not improvements are necessary.

These reviews need to make use of records such as:
- Customer satisfaction surveys
- Service and process performance, usually measured through Key Performance Indicators (KPIs)
- Resource usage reports
- Personnel performance, usually measured through individual performance and (potential) expertise, experience and knowledge gaps
- Organizational risk assessment results
- (Internal) Audit results
- Status of improvement actions, corrective actions and actions as a result of previous reviews
- Major (organizational, market, or service) changes on the horizon

Executive management is required to keep records of its decisions and actions as a result of these reviews.

(4.5.5) Maintain and improve the SMS (Act)

(4.5.5.1) General
During this phase of the service quality improvement cycle the service provider keeps the quality circle spinning by continuously looking for opportunities for improvement. A policy and a procedure in support of this effort are required by the standard. The procedure needs to specify the roles and responsibilities of those involved with identifying, documenting, evaluating, prioritizing, approving, managing, measuring and reporting on the improvements. These activities describe what in many organizations is called a Continual Service Improvement (CSI) process, model, approach or procedure.

Note that corrective and preventative actions are also considered opportunities for improvement. Clause 8.5 of ISO 9001:2008 "Measurement, analysis and improvement" provides more information on these actions.

8.5 (5) Design and transition of new or changed services

(5.1) General
The standard expects the service provider to use this process for all new services or changed services with the potential to have a major impact on customers or services. A change to a service is usually considered a major change. Major changes require intense customer involvement. Service providers often use project management approaches to manage such changes and assure that customer communication is covered from the very beginning until after the service change is operational. The standard requires that major changes to the Change Management policy

and associated processes are addressed and agreed upon by the appropriate parties.

In practice, this means that the service provider's project or program management practice needs to synchronize its activities with the organization's change management process practices. This includes synchronization with the application software development, Application Management, the Release and Deployment Management process practices, and the IT operations practices. And when adding to this mix that traditionally there is a gap between the development and operations sides of the "IT-house", the stage has been set for the challenge ahead. Through strong executive management involvement this challenge can be dealt with successfully. Success is accelerated by establishing an end-to-end mindset which can be considered as a prerequisite for success regarding this section of the standard.

Besides the Change Management process's involvement with the design and transition of new or changed service process, Configuration Management involvement is required. All the Configuration Items (CIs) that are affected by the service change need to be controlled by the Configuration Management process.

In addition, a usually undefined Requirements Management process or approach would benefit meeting the requirements of the design and transition of new or changed service process. The standard requires that the outcomes of the new or changed services meet the customer requirements. Through a continuous monitoring and reviewing effort throughout the design, development and deployment phases of a new or changed service project that compares the service requirements with the

outcomes of each phase, the chances of the customer accepting
the outputs of the design and transition of new or changed service
process will increase.

Note that requests for new services or changes to services can
originate from not only customers. The service provider, an
internal support team or a supplier can also be the reason for
these kinds of major changes.

8.6   (5.2) Plan new or changed services

The standard requires that the service provider determines the
requirements of a service change, that the service provider plans
how to meet those requirements and that the service provider
seeks agreement with the stakeholders on those plans.

The plans for these service changes need to include the financial,
organizational and technical consequences of the new or changed
service as well as the possible impact on the SMS. For example,
the new or changed service may require that some procedures or
work instructions need to be adjusted, which in turn could affect
some process interfaces or a knowledge gap that needs to be
addressed. Not to mention when SLAs, documented agreements
between internal parties, and/or Supplier Contracts need to be
modified, or new service reports need to be implemented.

The planning activities for a new or changed service will need to
include:
- The roles, responsibilities and authorities of all involved with
  the design, development and deployment efforts
- How all parties involved will communicate throughout the
  project
- The resources and timelines to be considered

- How the organizational risks will be analyzed, assessed and managed throughout the project
- How other services might be affected
- How the new or changed service will be tested, accepted and measured on meeting the service requirements

Note that a changed service also may include the decommissioning of a service. The standard addressed specific requirements for such services.

The service provider also needs to take into account in its planning efforts that other parties may need to be involved with the delivery of the new or changed service. The standard mentions requirements to assure these other parties have the capability to do the job in accordance with the defined policies and procedures.

8.7 (5.3) Design and development of new or changed services

Designing and developing new or changed services is about executing the plan(s) as described in the previous section of the standard. The service provider has to provide evidence (documents and records) of:

- Roles, responsibilities and authorities involved with the service delivery efforts that have been assigned to the appropriate parties including the customer, the service provider and other parties in such a way that each knows which activities they need to execute
- Resource requirements for the service delivery, including people, financial, and technology resources

- New or changed versions of documents such as policies, plans, Service Catalog, SLAs, Supplier Contracts, procedures, and KPIs; or changes to the SMS in general.

Note that Clause 7.3 of ISO 9001:2008 provides more information about the design and development process. You can find additional guidance in Clause 6.4.3 of the ISO/IEC 15288:2008 standard. This clause describes the architectural design process.

8.8   (5.4) Transition of new or changed services

As with every change, service changes need to be tested throughout the development phase and certainly before they become operational. This section of the standard requires such testing, as well as making sure that the outputs of the design and development of new or changed service processes meet the requirements and acceptance criteria of all involved, the customer, the service provider and other parties (e.g. suppliers).

The Release and Deployment Management process is to be used to perform these tests and verifications and to eventually, after approval, deploy the new or changed service.

Given the breadth of such deployment, the typical Release and Deployment Management process may need to be enhanced. The scope of the traditional Release and Deployment Management process includes software releases. More elaborate versions also include infrastructure releases. However, the standard requires more when considering the requirements in the planning, design and development of new services. For example, the service provider's personnel need to be included in these test and verification efforts. This means: "Is the IT operations staff ready to maintain, monitor, review and improve (when needed) the new or changed service?" In other words, do your acceptance criteria include a checklist for the IT operations staff to sign off on? Or, in another example, have earlier identified knowledge gaps been bridged through training and education before going live?

After going live the service provider needs to report on the quality of the service deployed in comparison with what was required from the outset of the project.

Predominant[1] process interfaces of the design and development of new or changed services process are (in order of appearance in the standard):
- Service Level Management
- Service Reporting
- Budgeting and Accounting for Services
- Business Relationship Management
- Supplier Management
- Configuration Management
- Change Management
- Release and Deployment Management

8.9   (6) Service delivery processes
- The Service delivery process set includes the following processes:
- Service Level Management
- Service Reporting
- Service Continuity and Availability Management
- Budgeting and Accounting for Services

---

1   Other process interfaces may apply

- Capacity Management
- Information Security Management

(6.1) Service Level Management

The service provider's services within the scope of certification are designed, developed and deployed through the design and development of new or changed services process. The Service Level Management process interfaces with this process. It is the responsibility of the Service Level Management process to monitor the performance of the service levels and compare those with the agreed upon service level targets.

While this may seem a straightforward effort, in practice it is not that easy. First of all, for each service level the service provider needs to identify the work involved - that is, the process (or processes) involved to meet the expected level of service. The table below lists a few examples of service levels and the processes involved to meet the expected level of service (Table 8.1).

Table 8.1 Examples of service levels and processes to meet expected level of service

Service level	Processes directly involved to meet the service level (other processes may be involved indirectly)
Call response time	Incident and Service Request Management Problem Management
Service availability	Service Continuity and Availability Management Capacity Management Information Security Management
Service window	Incident and Service Request Management Change Management Release and Deployment Management
Cost of service	Budgeting and accounting of services Configuration Management

Service level	Processes directly involved to meet the service level (other processes may be involved indirectly)
Disaster recovery service (e.g. Recovery Time Objective (RTO) and Recovery Point Objective (RPO)	Service Continuity and Availability Management Capacity Management Information Security Management Configuration Management
Service reviews	Service Reporting Business Relationship Management Supplier Management

Before agreeing to requested service level targets, the appropriate service provider's Process Owners will need to come to an agreement whether or not such service level can be delivered. These efforts will highly benefit from making each service level SMART (Specific, Measureable, Achievable, Realistic, Time-bound). By making each service level measurable, the monitoring requirement of the standard can be met.

The standard further requires that the service provider has a Service Catalog and Service Level Agreements for the services within the scope of ISO/IEC 20000 certification. These need to be agreed upon with the customer and be frequently reviewed with the customer.

The standard continues by mentioning requirements involving changes to the Service Catalog or the SLAs. Considering the table above, such changes should only be made in a controlled manner. Which better process than the Change Management process is best suited for such (service) changes? Therefore, these kinds of changes need the involvement of the Change Management process according to the standard.

Operational Level Agreements (OLAs), agreements between departments of the same organization, are not defined in the standard and are therefore not mentioned in it. However, the Service Level Management process makes references to similar type of agreements, but calls it simply a documented agreement. It requires the service provider to have documented agreements with internal groups providing service components in support of the service provider's services. A crucial component of these SLAs and the documented agreements are the process interfaces between the two parties. By addressing the process interfaces, the alignment of the service level targets of all the agreements involved will have a better success rate.

As with every process in the standard, the Service Level Management process includes requirements involving the determination of room for process improvements. Process specific KPIs and the performance levels compared with these KPIs can be of help when determining these opportunities for process improvement. Such identified improvements are fed into the service improvement procedure as required by the *Maintain and improve the SMS (Act)* requirements of the standard.

Predominant[2] process interfaces of the Service Level Management process are (in order of appearance in the standard):
- Change Management is the only process specifically referenced by the standard in this section. However, considering the statement made about how each service level needs the backing of at least one other process, it is fair to say that the Service Level Management process interfaces closely with every other process of the standard.

---

2 Other process interfaces may apply

(6.2) Service Reporting

The Service Reporting process outputs provide insight on the performance of every service delivered by the service provider, the service provider's SMS and every process of the standard. For example, the monitoring results of every service level need to be reported on. Or the KPIs of every process need to be reported on. The Service Reporting process provides these reports.

The standard mentions in high level terms some additional examples the service provider should at least generate reports of:

- Performance levels indicating how the service provider handled major incidents, major service changes and disasters
- Service demand and service usage levels
- Trends in Incidents, Problems, Changes, Releases, service availability, breaches, etc.
- Customer satisfaction levels
- Levels of compliance with and adherence to requirements of the standard, service requirements, SMS requirements, legal and statutory requirements

Since these service reports are often records which serve as evidence of the service provider's intentions, the standard's requirements for such records apply. The standard goes one step further by requiring that for each report some metadata needs to be documented. Examples of such metadata are the name of each report, the reason this report is being generated, the frequency of generating the report, the target audience and distribution list of the report and data sources the report uses to pull its data from.

The standard also requires that the service provider is actually doing something with the reports. Documented decisions, action items and communication records serve as evidence to meet this requirement.

Predominant[3] Process Interfaces of the Service Reporting process (in order of appearance in the standard):

* Only references to the design and implementation of new or changed service processes, the Service Continuity and Availability Management process and the Incident Management process are made in this section by the standard. However, considering the standard's requirement that the Service Reporting process generates reports for all processes, it is fair to say that the Service Reporting interfaces closely with every other process of the standard.

(6.3) Service Continuity and Availability Management

(6.3.1) Service continuity and availability requirements

So far the standard has only required a Risk Management process/model/approach for dealing with organizational risks. Having a Risk Management process/model/approach for dealing with risks involving aspects such as threats, vulnerabilities, disasters, mitigation and recovery will be beneficial to meeting the requirements of this process. Note that the standard does not require having a Risk Management process/model/approach for these kinds of risks. However, the typical activities performed when managing such risks are referenced by the standard such as identifying the risks, assessing the risks and agreeing on how to respond to these risks. Each of these activities has to use business plans, service requirements, and SLAs as a reference when determining and assessing the risks and risk mitigations.

---

3 Other process interfaces may apply

(6.3.2) Service continuity and availability plans

The service provider is required to develop, deploy and maintain a service continuity plan, or plans, and an availability plan, or plans. These plans are based on input provided by other parts and processes of the standard. For example, customer needs, market developments, service requirements, legal and statutory requirements, etc.

Considering the breadth and depth of topics to be addressed in the plans, the impact of making changes to these plans can be significant (e.g. recovery procedures and service availability targets in the event of a disaster). To assure these changes are being made in a controlled manner the standard requires the involvement of the Change Management process. Changes to these plans can be the result of a review of the plan(s) which needs to be done frequently according to the standard. Typical review points are when introducing new or changed services or when test results of the service continuity plan require changes to the plan(s). Furthermore, any request for change may potentially have an impact on the plan(s). This is why the standard requires that when assessing a change in the Change Management process, the possible impact on these plans needs to be considered.

(6.3.3) Service continuity and availability monitoring and testing

According to the standard, the service provider is required to measure and report on the availability of the service(s) within the scope of certification. This is easier said than done, considering that a service consists of components which may cause challenges to measure them (e.g. human resources). At the same time the IT industry has evolved over the years and end-to-end service availability monitoring tools have become available for systems used in many IT environments (e.g. Enterprise Resource Planning - ERP systems) and are capable of measuring the technology components of a service. Besides human and technology service components the process performance is an important service component to be measured from an availability perspective.

It is a requirement to investigate whichever component(s) contributed to an unplanned non-availability of a service and to take the appropriate actions to avoid a repeat of such outage.

Both the service continuity and the availability plan(s), need to be tested frequently. The results of these tests need to be recorded and if a follow up action is required, the service provider needs to show evidence of this (e.g. change records).

Predominant[4] process interfaces of the Service Continuity and Availability Management process are (in order of appearance in the standard):
- Design and implement new or changed services process
- Service Level Management
- Service Reporting
- Configuration Management
- Change Management

(6.4) Budgeting and Accounting for Services

It is common that the service provider's organization has a Financial Management department performing the various activities involved with this ISO/IEC 20000 process. The service provider is therefore required to determine the interfaces of its

---

4   Other process interfaces may apply

Budgeting and Accounting for Services process and the processes in place in the Financial Management department, or the rest of the organization for that matter.

Given that business decisions may be influenced by financial issues, it is to be expected that the standard requires a tight interface between the Budgeting and Accounting for Services process and the Financial Management process of the service provider's organization. By integrating both processes, the service provider should be able to make use of the practices that are already in place which contribute to meeting the ISO/IEC 20000 requirements.

The standard is very specific when listing the requirements for the policy, or policies, and for the procedure(s) supporting the Budgeting and Accounting for Services process. For example, the service components to be addressed in the policy and the procedure are specifically spelled out (e.g. financial assets, resources, expenses, and third party services).

Also, the policy and associated procedures must address the apportionment of costs and cost allocation, as well as the controls and approvals involved with the process.

Furthermore, the process needs to address the budgeting, monitoring, review of costs and the reporting activities involved as well as the management of it all.

And finally, the Budgeting and Accounting for Services process needs to support the assessment activity from a costing perspective of the Change Management process.

Predominant[5] process interfaces of the Budgeting and Accounting for Services process are (in order of appearance in the standard):

- Design and implement new or changed services process
- Service Level Management
- Service Reporting
- Supplier Management
- Configuration Management
- Change Management

(6.5) Capacity Management

The development, deployment and maintenance of a Capacity Plan are the main activities of this process according to the standard. In order to obtain the appropriate information the plan needs to be based on identified and agreed capacity and performance requirements. These inputs for the process come from the customer, from the service provider and from suppliers. The Capacity Plan not only addresses technology-related capacity aspects, but also resources such as people and financial aspects as well as current and future information demands.

The standard is very specific about what the Capacity Plan needs to address. In generic terms the Plan covers:

- Service usage demands, anticipated service usage patterns and trends
- Impact on capacity needs based on agreed availability, continuity and service levels such as support windows and performance requirements

---

5 Other process interfaces may apply

- Impact on capacity needs based on legal and statutory requirements and anticipated new or changed services and changes in general
- Cost details related to meeting the capacity requirements

Any changes to the Capacity Plan need to be handled in a controlled manner and therefore follow the Change Management process.

In addition, the service provider is required to monitor, measure, and analyze capacity usage data to enable optimal tuning of the service performance in such a way that agreed upon capacity and performance requirements can be met.

Predominant[6] process interfaces of the Capacity Management process are (in order of appearance in the standard):
- Design and implement new or changed services process
- Service Level Management
- Service Reporting
- Service Continuity and Availability Management
- Budgeting and Accounting for Services
- Supplier Management
- Configuration Management
- Change Management

(6.6) Information Security Management
In Chapter 6.2 of this book you will find an overview of how meeting the Information Security Management process requirements can benefit from the ISO/IEC 27001 standard for Information Security Management.

---

6 Other process interfaces may apply

(6.6.1) Information security policy

Besides security requirements that are part of service requirements, the Information Security Management process needs to take into account any legal and statutory requirements. By implementing appropriate policies and controls these requirements can be met. The ISO/IEC 27002, the Code of Practice for Information Security Management, is more specific about the information security policy. Examples of what the ISO/IEC 20000 standard requires from a policy perspective are:

- The policy needs to be communicated to the appropriate parties
- The policy needs to make sure that information security requirements can be met
- The policy needs to describe how information security risks are analyzed and assessed and how countermeasures are implemented and managed
- The policy needs to make sure that information security audits will be held and what needs to be done with the outcomes of these audits

(6.6.2) Information security controls

The ISO/IEC 27002 standard is more specific about the information security controls. Examples of information security controls referred to by the ISO/IEC 20000 are:

- Controls involving the confidentiality, integrity and accessibility of data, including access to the data by third parties
- Controls involving meeting the information security policy clauses
- Controls involving the management of information security risks

The service provider is required to document, maintain, review and, when necessary, improve these controls.

(6.6.3) Information security changes and incidents
The ISO/IEC 20000 standard requires that:
- The assessment of requests for changes take information security risks into account as well as their impact on the information security policy and controls
- Information security incidents follow the Incident Management procedures
- Information security incidents are reported on to determine any opportunity for improvement, to avoid a repetition of these incidents or minimize their impact

The ISO/IEC 27002 Code of Practice for Information Security Management is more specific about the information security controls involving changes and incidents.

Predominant[7] process interfaces of the Information Security Management process are (in order of appearance in the standard):
- Design and implement new or changed services process
- Service Level Management
- Service Reporting
- Service Continuity and Availability Management
- Supplier Management
- Incident Management
- Configuration Management
- Change Management

---

7 Other process interfaces may apply

8.10 (7) Relationship processes

The relationship process set includes the following processes:

- Business Relationship Management
- Supplier Management

The diagram below (Figure 8.4) shows how the Business Relationship Management process, the Service Level Management process and the Supplier Management process cooperate with each other. The Business Relationship Management process acts as the "face of the service provider" and assures that at a strategic level the service provider:

- Understands the business and its current and future needs
- Understands the capabilities and constraints
- Understands the responsibilities and obligations

The Supplier Management process is responsible for communicating these same aspects with the suppliers and assuring that they are understood.

The Service Level Management is the linking pin between the relationship processes and translates the needs of the business into services and service levels to be implemented and managed by the service provider and appropriately supported by the applicable suppliers.

The challenge the service provider is confronted with is conflicting policies, processes and procedures. All three processes are responsible for identifying these discrepancies and responding accordingly. Vehicles to assure the synchronization of policies, processes and procedures are Service Level Agreement (SLAs) with customers, supported by Underpinning Contracts (UCs) or supplier contracts with suppliers and,

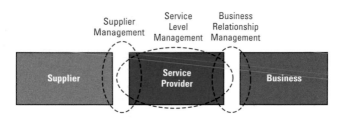

Figure 8.4 Cooperation between Business Relationship Management process, Service Level Management process and Supplier Management process

if applicable, supported by Operational Level Agreements (OLAs), or documented agreements as the standards calls these agreements, with supporting entities within the service provider's organization.

(7.1) Business Relationship Management

The main focus of the Business Relationship Management process is to keep the customer satisfied. The process enables the service provider to be proactive about meeting the customer's needs. Constant communication is crucial to accomplish this objective, which is why several requirements of the standard evolve around this aspect.

In order to communicate properly one needs to know who to communicate with. This explains the standard's requirements to determine and document the customer's contact persons, users and other stakeholders. Each customer needs to have assigned a dedicated contact person who represents the service provider.

Whenever the customer expresses the need for a new service or a change to an existing service, or, in an ideal scenario, the Business Relationship Management processes, proposes a new service or a change to an existing service with the customer's approval, the standard requires that these needs and associated service requirements are documented and controlled with the help of the Change Management process. Whenever these requirements affect (existing) service levels, the Service Level Management process has to be involved.

The Service Level Management and Service Reporting processes enable the requirement of frequently reviewing the service provider's performance with the customer. This includes documenting, responding to and handling customer complaints.

And finally, the Business Relationship Management process is required to act as a barometer to frequently measure the customer's satisfaction levels.

Predominant[8] process interfaces of the Business Relationship Management process are (in order of appearance in the standard):
- Design and implement new or changed services process
- Service Level Management
- Service Reporting
- Change Management

(7.2) Supplier Management
The main focus of the Supplier Management process is to assure that the suppliers perform as agreed upon in support of the services and service levels agreed with the service provider's customer(s). Constant communication between the service provider and the suppliers is needed to enable the achievement

---

8   Other process interfaces may apply

of this objective. Several requirements of the standard therefore address this communication aspect.

The standard distinguishes three types of suppliers:
- Suppliers
- Lead suppliers
- Subcontracted suppliers

Figure 8.5 positions each type of supplier in the supplier's service supply chain

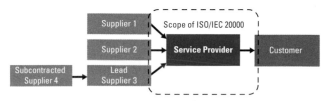

Figure 8.5 Types of supplier in the supplier's service supply chain

Suppliers deliver services to the service provider without depending on other suppliers. Lead suppliers, on the other hand, do depend on other suppliers. The latter type of supplier is therefore called a subcontracted supplier. A typical example of a lead supplier is a system integrator or an application service provider hosting applications and depending on hardware and network suppliers for the delivery of the application services.

When dealing with lead suppliers, the standard expects that the service provider's supplier contract describes the roles and the relationship between the lead supplier and the subcontracted supplier(s) as well as how the lead supplier manages the relationship with the subcontracted supplier(s).

ISO/IEC TR 20000-3 provides examples of supply chain relationships.

The ISO/IEC 20000-1 standard is very specific about what needs to be addressed in a Supplier Contract. Examples of clauses it requires are:

- The services, service level requirements, service level targets to be fulfilled by the supplier as well as the dependencies between the service provider's services and the supplier's services
- The processes operated by the supplier and the dependencies between the service provider's processes and the supplier's processes
- The integration between the service provider's SMS and the supplier's SMS including aspects such as communication, authorities, and responsibilities

From a process perspective the Service Level Management process is the linking pin between the Supplier Management and the Business Relationship Management processes. This means that the SLAs agreed upon with the customer need to be supported by the supplier contracts. It is the responsibility of the Supplier Management process to negotiate these contracts and to assure that they align with the SLAs with the customer. The Service Level Management process facilitates this effort by appropriately involving and informing the Supplier Management process.

Whenever a supplier contract requires to be changed the Change Management process is involved to ensure these changes will be handled in a controlled manner.

Predominant[9] process interfaces of the Supplier Management process are (in order of appearance in the standard):
- Service Level Management
- Budgeting and Accounting for Services
- Change Management

8.11   (8) Resolution processes

The Resolution process set includes the following processes:
- Incident and Service Request Management
- Problem Management

(8.1) Incident and Service Request Management

Although in name Incidents and Service Requests are part of the same process, the Incident and Service Request Management process, the management of Incidents and of Service Requests is done through different procedures. The reason for handling Incidents and Service Requests through different procedures is their nature. Service Requests do not need to be investigated, diagnosed, resolved, and recovered; Incidents do. Service Requests are recorded, fulfilled and closed.

Both Incidents and Service Requests need to be prioritized. The priority needs to be determined through establishing their impact and the urgency. The standard does not define impact and urgency, but in general the impact is expressed in the number of people, devices, or CIs that are affected and the urgency expresses the importance to the business of the particular Incident or Service Request.

---

9 Other process interfaces may apply

The handling of Incidents and of Service Requests benefits when those responsible for them have access to knowledge sources such as Workarounds, Known Errors, resolutions of past Incidents, Service Requests and of Problems, CI information, Release Plans, Rollout Plans, Release notes, etc.

The Incident and Service Request Management process is a predominantly customer-facing process. This is why the standard includes communication requirements such as keeping the customer informed at all times about the progress of the handling of the customer's Incidents and Service Requests.

A third procedure is required by the standard as part of the Incident and Service Request Management process. This involves the handling of major Incidents. The service provider is responsible for agreeing with the customer on the definition of a major Incident. The handling of such major Incidents requires the involvement of the service provider's executive management.

Predominant[10] process interfaces of the Incident and Service Request Management process are (in order of appearance in the standard):
- Service Level Management
- Problem Management
- Configuration Management
- Change Management
- Release and Deployment Management

---

10 Other process interfaces may apply

(8.2) Problem Management

Although on the surface the Problem Management process
follows similar steps compared to the handling of Incidents in the
Incident and Service Request Management process, the nature of
Problem Management is completely different. Incidents need to
be resolved as quickly as possible. The resolution of the majority
of Problems requires more time and multi-discipline resources.

With the objective to minimize the impact of Incidents or to
prevent Incidents from happening in the first place, it is Problem
Management's responsibility to determine Workarounds
(i.e. temporary solutions), root causes, and permanent solutions.
Workarounds and permanent solutions may require changes.
These changes need to be handled under the control of the
Change Management process.

The requirement to be preventative comes along with the
Problem Management process to be proactive. Data and
trend analyses requirements support this need for potential
preventative activities.

Given that knowledgeable staff are involved with the
Problem Management process the standard requires that this
accumulation of knowledge is shared with staff of the service
provider's organization who could benefit from it during the
fulfillment of their process duties. The Incident and Service
Request Management process is spelled out in particular by the
standard in this regard.

Predominant[11] process interfaces of the Problem Management
process are (in order of appearance in the standard):
* Service Reporting
* Incident and Service Request Management
* Configuration Management
* Change Management

8.12 (9) Control processes
The Control process set includes the following processes:
* Configuration Management
* Change Management
* Release and Deployment Management

(9.1) Configuration Management
Many processes benefit from the information provided by the
Configuration Management process - in particular, the Change
Management and the Release and Deployment Management
process. It is the responsibility of the Configuration Management
process to maintain and control accurate configuration
information of the components of the service provider's services
and its supporting infrastructure. The information provided by
Configuration Management to the Change Management process
assists the latter process with the impact assessment activity. The
Release and Deployment Management's rollout and rollback
activities benefit from the Configuration Management process
by having it create a baseline to fall back on in the event of an
unsuccessful release, for example.

---

11 Other process interfaces may apply

It is the service provider's responsibility to define Configuration Item (CI) types and to document what information needs to be recorded for each CI. Examples of such information are:

- CI attributes such as a unique identification, status, version and location
- CI relationships with other CIs and with Service CIs
- Related Change records, Problem records and Known Error records

Given the dependency of other processes on accurate information provided by the Configuration Management process, the standard requires the process to have the controls in place to ensure the reliability and accuracy of the CIs stored in a Configuration Management Database (CMDB)[12], including the controls involving the accessibility to the CMDB.

To further increase these information quality requirements, the standard requires that the service provider frequently conducts audits to determine any discrepancies and subsequent corrective actions. In addition, any changes to CIs need to be tracked and traced.

The Configuration Management process is also responsible for storing master copies of CIs in secure libraries - for example, hardware spares in a secure physical environment and authorized software in a secure electronic environment. The CMDB needs to reflect these CIs and the secure library they are stored in. Other examples of master copies are images of hardware configurations and documentation.

---

12 Note that a service provider may have multiple CMDBs.

Predominant[13] process interfaces of the Configuration
Management process are (in order of appearance in the
standard):
- Service Level Management
- Budgeting and Accounting for Services
- Information Security Management
- Problem Management
- Change Management
- Release and Deployment Management

(9.2) Change Management

The Change Management process is responsible for recording,
classifying, accepting, assessing, approving, scheduling, and
reviewing changes. It also ensures that approved changes are
implemented and tested. The latter activities are controlled by
the Release and Deployment process.

Not every Change is controlled by the Change Management
process. Major (service) Changes are to be controlled by the
Design and Transition of New or Changed Service process.
This may include the removal of a service or the transfer of a
service from one service provider to another. The criteria of
what constitutes a Major Change are to be defined by the service
provider.

Emergency Changes are to be controlled through a separate
Emergency Change procedure. The customer needs to agree to
what constitutes an Emergency Change.

---

13 Other process interfaces may apply

Definitions of Major Changes and Emergency Changes are to be documented in a Change Management Policy.

The assessment of Changes requires information from processes such as Configuration Management, Business Relationship Management, Supplier Management, and potentially of all the Service Delivery processes. Before approving the Change the risks and impact on the business, services, resources, and technology need to be taken into account, as well as the anticipated benefits for the customer. This effort may require a business case in support of it.

Once approved, the Change needs to be planned. This plan is often referred as a Change Schedule. This is to be communicated to all parties who need to know such as the customer, the relevant service provider's staff and the applicable supplier(s). The Release and Deployment Management process will base its Release Plan on this Change Schedule.

Part of the Change planning activity is the planning, and if possible the testing, of a Remediation Plan or Fallback Plan.

The CMDB needs to reflect every Change that was implemented successfully. This is another example of the close cooperation between the Change Management process and the Configuration Management process.

It is the responsibility of the Change Management process to investigate unsuccessful changes and determine which actions to take to avoid a future repeat of such change. Furthermore, the process needs to determine improvements in general to increase the number of successful Changes and the effectiveness of the process as a whole.

Predominant[14] process interfaces of the Change Management process are (in order of appearance in the standard):

- Service Level Management
- Service Reporting
- Configuration Management
- Release and Deployment Management

(9.3) Release and Deployment Management

The Release and Deployment Management process is responsible for creating a Release Policy. This policy defines:

- The types of Releases (e.g. Major Release, Minor Release, Emergency Release) and a definition for each type
- The frequency of Releases (e.g. bi-annually, weekly)

The customer needs to be involved with the development of this Release Policy. The service provider is required to come to an agreement with the customer on the policy.

Another major output of the Release and Deployment Management process is the Release Plan. This plan is not to be confused with the Deployment or Rollout Plan. The latter plan describes in great detail the steps involved with deploying or rolling out a Release. Part of the Deployment or Rollout planning activity is the planning, and if possible the testing, of a Remediation Plan or Fallback Plan.

---

14 Other process interfaces may apply

The Release Plan on the other hand is more high-level and describes deployment dates, deliverables and deployment methods (e.g. automated and manual Releases). This Release Plan is developed in a combined effort with the customer, the applicable service provider's staff and supplier(s) and with the Change Management process. The Release Plan is to be shared with the Incident and Service Request Management process.

Emergency Releases need to be managed through a separate procedure by the service provider. This procedure needs to interface with the Emergency Change procedure of the Change Management process.

Releases need to be built and tested before going live. A controlled acceptance test environment is required in support of this effort. Furthermore, the service provider needs to agree on the acceptance criteria with the customer(s) and the applicable service provider's staff and supplier(s) before putting a Release in production. In most cases this is an iterative effort.

Besides an accepted Release, the success of the Release is also determined by the degree to which the Release was able to maintain the integrity of the Service and all its components during the deployment phase. A way to measure this level of integrity is by measuring the number of Incidents that are a direct result of the Release.

A third way of declaring a Release as a success is by determining the level of impact the Release had on the customer for example, by avoiding any unplanned downtime.

Unsuccessful Releases need to be investigated to avoid a future repeat. Opportunities for improvement need to be determined and agreed upon.

Predominant[15] process interfaces of the Release and Deployment Management process (in order of appearance in the standard):

- Service Level Management
- Service Reporting
- Supplier Management
- Incident and Service Request Management
- Problem Management
- Configuration Management
- Change Management

---

15 Other process interfaces may apply

9 ISO/IEC 20000 self-assessment

9.1 Preparation

Through the following eight-step approach you can conduct a self-assessment to determine your level of compliance with the requirements of the ISO/IEC 20000-1:2011 standard:

1. Obtain a copy of the ISO/IEC 20000-1:2011 standard and familiarize yourself with the requirements.
2. In case these are your first steps in the IT Service Management field of expertise, and in order to better interpret the requirements of the standard it is highly recommended to:
   a. Attend and successfully complete a Foundation level certification training course
   b. Purchase and read additional IT Service Management and/or ISO/IEC 20000 publications
   c. Research the Internet and read additional IT Service Management and/or ISO/IEC 20000 white papers, presentations, etc.
3. Create an assessment document consisting of a table that could look as follows (Table 9.1).

Table 9.1 Example assessment document

#	ISO/IEC 20000 Requirement	Answer (Y/N)	Evidence: Document	Evidence: Record
1	The service provider shall create, implement and maintain a Service Management plan.		Service Management Plan	Audit trail of updates to the Service Management Plan

#	ISO/IEC 20000 Requirement	Answer (Y/N)	Evidence: Document	Evidence: Record
2	Plans created for specific processes shall be aligned with the Service Management plan.		Process Plans	Process Owners Meeting Minutes and Alignment Action Items
3	Etc.			

4. Choose an assessment scope by determining those services most likely to be included in the eventual scope of ISO/IEC 20000 certification. Take this scope into account when establishing a team of interviewees, ideally consisting of Executive Management, Relationship Managers, Line Managers, Process Owners, Service Owners, Subject Matter Experts, etc.

9.2   Assessment and reporting

5. Conduct the interviews in a short and comprehensive timeframe. When in doubt answer a question with "No". Or when almost meeting the requirement, still answer with a "No". Remember, an audit requires that you meet all the requirements of the standard.

6. Collect your results and share it in a diagram that could look like this (Figure 9.1).

9.3   Review and act

1. Collectively, with all the parties involved determine those gaps that can be closed with relatively little effort and those that need priority. Define a small improvement project for those gaps that require more time and effort.

2. It is useful to benefit from guidance provided by additional:
   a. ISO/IEC 20000 documents (e.g. part 2 through 5);

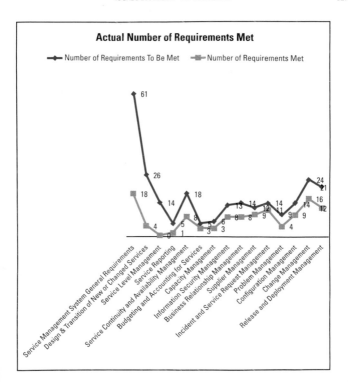

Figure 9.1 Results diagram

   b. Literature as referenced in chapter 1.2 of this book;

   c. Certification training; and maybe even from consulting
      services when closing the gaps.

3. By repeating this self-assessment you can keep score of your
   progress. Make sure to communicate the achievements and
   celebrate your improvements.

Annex A Glossary: terminology and definitions

The terms and definitions defined in ISO/IEC 20000-1:2011 are listed below.

TERM	ISO/IEC 20000 DEFINITION
Availability	ability of a service or service component to perform its required function at an agreed instant or over an agreed period of time *NOTE: Availability is normally expressed as a ratio or percentage of the time that the service or service component is actually available for use by the customer to the agreed time that the service should be available.*
Configuration baseline	configuration information formally designated at a specific time during a service or service component's life *NOTE 1: Configuration baselines, plus approved changes from those baselines, constitute the current configuration information.* *NOTE 2: Adapted from ISO/IEC/IEEE 24765:2010.*
Configuration Item (CI)	element that needs to be controlled in order to deliver a service or services
Configuration Management Database (CMDB)	data store used to record attributes of configuration items, and the relationships between configuration items, throughout their lifecycle
Continual improvement	recurring activity to increase the ability to fulfil service requirements
Corrective action	action to eliminate the cause or reduce the likelihood of recurrence of a detected nonconformity or other undesirable situation *NOTE: Adapted from ISO 9000:2005.*

TERM	ISO/IEC 20000 DEFINITION
Customer	organization or part of an organization that receives a service or services *NOTE 1: A customer can be internal or external to the service provider's organization.* *NOTE 2: Adapted from ISO 9000:2005.*
Document	information and its supporting medium *[ISO 9000:2005]* *EXAMPLES: Policies, plans, process descriptions, procedures, service level agreements, contracts or records.* *NOTE 1: The documentation can be in any form or type of medium.* *NOTE 2: In ISO/IEC 20000, documents, except for records, state the intent to be achieved.*
Effectiveness	extent to which planned activities are realized and planned results achieved *[ISO 9000:2005]*
Incident	unplanned interruption to a service, a reduction in the quality of a service or an event that has not yet impacted the service to the customer
Information security	preservation of confidentiality, integrity and accessibility of information *NOTE 1: In addition, other properties such as authenticity, accountability, non-repudiation and reliability can also be involved.* *NOTE 2: The term "availability" has not been used in this definition because it is a defined term in this part of*

TERM	ISO/IEC 20000 DEFINITION
	ISO/IEC 20000 which would not be appropriate for this definition. *NOTE 3: Adapted from ISO/IEC 27000:2009.*
Information security incident	single or a series of unwanted or unexpected information security events that have a significant probability of compromising business operations and threatening information security *[ISO/IEC 27000:2009]*
Interested party	person or group having a specific interest in the performance or success of the service provider's activity or activities *EXAMPLES: Customers, owners, management, people in the service provider's organization, suppliers, bankers, unions or partners.* *NOTE 1: A group can comprise an organization, a part thereof, or more than one organization.* *NOTE 2: Adapted from ISO 9000:2005.*
Internal group	part of the service provider's organization that enters into a documented agreement with the service provider to contribute to the design, transition, delivery and improvement of a service or services *NOTE: The internal group is outside the scope of the service provider's Service Management System.*
Known error	problem that has an identified root cause or a method of reducing or eliminating its impact on a service by working around it
Nonconformity	non-fulfillment of a requirement *[ISO 9000:2005]*

TERM	ISO/IEC 20000 DEFINITION
Organization	group of people and facilities with an arrangement of responsibilities, authorities and relationships *EXAMPLES: Company, corporation, firm, enterprise, institution, charity, sole trader, association, or parts or combination thereof.* *NOTE 1: The arrangement is generally orderly.* *NOTE 2: An organization can be public or private.* *[ISO 9000:2005]*
Preventive action	action to avoid or eliminate the causes or reduce the likelihood of occurrence of a potential nonconformity or other potential undesirable situation *NOTE: Adapted from ISO 9000:2005.*
Problem	root cause of one or more incidents *NOTE: The root cause is not usually known at the time a problem record is created and the problem management process is responsible for further investigation.*
Procedure	specified way to carry out an activity or a process *[ISO 9000:2005]* *NOTE: Procedures can be documented or not.*
Process	set of interrelated or interacting activities which transforms inputs into outputs *[ISO 9000:2005]*
Record	document stating results achieved or providing evidence of activities performed *[ISO 9000:2005]*

TERM	ISO/IEC 20000 DEFINITION
	EXAMPLES: Audit reports, incident reports, training records or minutes of meetings.
Release	collection of one or more new or changed configuration items deployed into the live environment as a result of one or more changes
Request for change	proposal for a change to be made to a service, service component or the SMS *NOTE: A change to a service includes the provision of a new service or the removal of a service which is no longer required.*
Risk	effect of uncertainty on objectives *NOTE 1: An effect is a deviation from the expected — positive and/or negative.* *NOTE 2: Objectives can have different aspects (such as financial, health and safety, and environmental goals) and can apply at different levels (such as strategic, organization-wide, project, product and process).* *NOTE 3: Risk is often characterized by reference to potential events and consequences, or a combination of these.* *NOTE 4: Risk is often expressed in terms of a combination of the consequences of an event (including changes in circumstances) and the associated likelihood of occurrence.* *[ISO 31000:2009]*
Service	means of delivering value for the customer by facilitating results the customer wants to achieve *NOTE 1: Service is generally intangible.*

TERM	ISO/IEC 20000 DEFINITION
	NOTE 2: A service can also be delivered to the service provider by a supplier, an internal group or a customer acting as a supplier.
Service component	single unit of a service that when combined with other units will deliver a complete service *EXAMPLES: Hardware, software, tools, applications, documentation, information, processes or supporting services.* *NOTE: A service component can consist of one or more configuration items.*
Service continuity	capability to manage risks and events that could have serious impact on a service or services in order to continually deliver services at agreed levels
Service Level Agreement (SLA)	documented agreement between the service provider and customer that identifies services and service targets *NOTE 1: A service level agreement can also be established between the service provider and a supplier, an internal group or a customer acting as a supplier.* *NOTE 2: A service level agreement can be included in a contract or another type of documented agreement.*
Service management	set of capabilities and processes to direct and control the service provider's activities and resources for the design, transition, delivery and improvement of services to fulfill the service requirements
Service Management system	management system to direct and control the Service Management activities of the service provider *NOTE 1: A management system is a set of interrelated or interacting elements to establish policy and objectives and to achieve those objectives.*

TERM	ISO/IEC 20000 DEFINITION
	NOTE 2: The SMS includes all Service Management policies, objectives, plans, processes, documentation and resources required for the design, transition, delivery and improvement of services and to fulfill the requirements in this part of ISO/IEC 20000. *NOTE 3: Adapted from the definition of "quality management system" in ISO 9000:2005.*
Service provider	organization or part of an organization that manages and delivers a service or services to the customer *NOTE: A customer can be internal or external to the service provider's organization.*
Service request	request for information, advice, access to a service or a pre-approved change
Service requirement	needs of the customer and the users of the service, including service level requirements, and the needs of the service provider
Supplier	organization or part of an organization that is external to the service provider's organization and enters into a contract with the service provider to contribute to the design, transition, delivery and improvement of a service or services or processes *NOTE: Suppliers include designated lead suppliers but not their sub-contracted suppliers.*
Top management	person or group of people who direct and control the service provider at the highest level *NOTE: Adapted from ISO 9000:2005.*
Transition	activities involved in moving a new or changed service to or from the live environment

ISO/IEC 20000:2011 – A Pocket Guide

Annex B
ISO/IEC 20000-1:2011 changes

With the release of the ISO/IEC 20000-1:2011 document several noteworthy changes compared to the 2005 edition are described in this chapter.

B.1 Name change

The ISO/IEC 20000-1:2011 document is now called "Service management system requirements" and no longer "Specification". This name change emphasizes that it is the Service Management System (SMS) that is being certified. More details of the standard's SMS are described below.

B.2 Changes in structure and size

The update to the ISO/IEC 20000:2011 version of the standard has come with changes to the structure and the size of the standard. Structurally, several sections have been combined, expanded and/or renamed.

Figure 5.1 shows the components of the 2011 edition of the ISO/IEC 20000-1 standard. In size the new edition has grown in the number of requirements from 170 to 256 when counting the "shall" statements, and from 16 to 25 pages. The table below provides a high level comparison of the number of requirements and sections of both versions (Table 5.1).

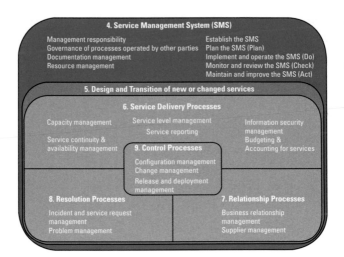

Figure B.1 Components of the 2011 edition of the ISO/IEC 20000-1 standard

Table B.1 High level comparison of both versions of the standard

ISO/IEC 20000:2011	# of Shalls	ISO/IEC 20000:2005	# of Shalls
1 Scope 1.1 General 1.2 Application	N/A	1 Scope	N/A
2 Normative References	N/A		
3 Terms and Definitions	N/A	2 Terms and Definitions	N/A
4 Service management system general requirements 4.1 Management responsibility 4.2 Governance of processes operated by other parties 4.3 Documentation management 4.4 Resource management	61	3 Requirements for a management system 3.1 Management responsibility	30

ISO/IEC 20000:2011	# of Shalls	ISO/IEC 20000:2005	# of Shalls
4.5 Establish and improve the SMS Establish the scope, Plan, Do, Check, Act		3.2 Documentation requirements 3.3 Competence, awareness and training 4 Planning and implementing Service Management Plan, Do, Check, Act	
5 Design and transition of new or changed services 5.1 General 5.2 Plan new or changed services 5.3 Design and development of new or changed services 5.4 Transition of new or changed services	26	5 Planning and implementing new or changed services	7
6 Service delivery processes 6.1 Service Level Management 6.2 Service Reporting 6.3 Service Continuity and Availability Management 6.4 Budgeting and Accounting for Services 6.5 Capacity Management 6.6 Information Security Management	61	6 Service delivery processes 6.1 Service Level Management 6.2 Service Reporting 6.3 Service Continuity and Availability Management 6.4 Budgeting and accounting for IT services 6.5 Capacity Management 6.6 Information Security Management	44

ISO/IEC 20000:2011	# of Shalls	ISO/IEC 20000:2005	# of Shalls
7 Relationship processes 7.1 Business Relationship Management 7.2 Supplier Management	26	7 Relationship processes 7.1 General 7.2 Business Relationship Management 7.3 Supplier Management	28
8 Resolution processes 8.1 Incident and Service Request Management 8.2 Problem Management	23	8 Resolution processes 8.1 Background 8.2 Incident Management 8.3 Problem Management	14
9 Control processes 9.1 Configuration Management 9.2 Change Management 9.3 Release and Deployment Management	59	9 Control processes 9.1 Configuration Management 9.2 Change Management 10.1 Release management	47
Total number of shall's	256	Total number of shall's	170

B.3   Integrated Management System

One of the reasons to publish a new version of the standard is to better align ISO/IEC 20000 with the ISO 9001 standard for Quality Management and with the Information Security Management standard, ISO/IEC 27001. This alignment has been achieved very well by allowing for an integration of the management systems of each standard. See Figure B.2 below.

A management system is a framework of policies, processes, procedures, guidelines and associated resources to achieve the objectives of an organization.

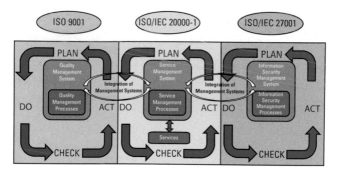

Figure B.2 Integrating the management systems of the standards

Each standard has its own management system. However, some fundamental components of these management systems are very similar - in particular, the requirements addressing:

- Management responsibility; e.g. management commitment, communication, top management's active involvement
- Documentation requirements; e.g. creation and control of documents and records
- Resource management; e.g. staff competencies, skills, and training
- Planning, implementing, reviewing and improving the management system - the plan-do-check-act methodology

When considering becoming ISO/IEC 20000 certified, meeting the Service Management System requirements is what the certification efforts are all about. The sooner the requirements of these fundamental components are being met, however, the smoother the efforts will be to meet the remaining requirements involving processes, procedures, process policies and service improvements. In Chapter 8 the requirements for the Service Management System are described in greater detail.

B.4   Other noticeable changes

Other noticeable changes between both versions of the ISO/IEC 20000 standard are listed below (Table B.2).

Table B.2 Other noticeable differences between the versions of the standard

ISO/IEC 20000-1:2005	ISO/IEC 20000-1:2011
The phrase "customer requirement"...	... has been replaced by "customer requirements and business needs".
A member of management...	... is now referred to as a management representative.
"Annual" review of plans...	... has been replaced by "at planned intervals"...
The phrase "stakeholders"...	... has been replaced by "interested parties".
The title "contract manager"...	... has been replaced by "designated individual who is responsible for managing the supplier".
The phrase "Management shall"...	... is still there, but now the standard also frequently refers to "The service provider shall".
For each process the objective of the process is given.	No process objective is given.

B.5   Major non-process-specific differences

Some differences in requirements of the 2011 edition of the standard that are not specific to a particular process and that stand out are:

1. Introduction of the term Service Management System

- In the 2005 version of the standard it was implied that it was the management system that was being audited for certification. The new version introduces the term Service Management System (SMS) and makes the management system a much more explicit part of the standard's requirements. It emphasizes that the focal point is the management system of services. A benefit of this new term is that it reduces the misconception that IT Service Management is mostly about implementing and improving processes (i.e. process improvement/management). While managing services requires the management of processes, there is more involved when managing services. Also, the elements such as the management of people, including the service provider's management and staff, as well as its suppliers, and the management of technology are crucial for successful service support and service delivery. Managing each of these elements in a coherent and systematic fashion is what is meant by a system approach to management as referred to by one of the eight principles of Quality Management as mentioned in chapter 2.3. Ignoring an element may decrease the quality of service.

- In the 2005 version of the standard Deming's Quality Circle was used for the planning and implementation of Service Management. In the new version the Circle is used to plan (Plan), implement and operate (Do), monitor and review (Check), and maintain and improve (Act) the Service Management System (SMS), the Service Management processes and the services. For each step a number of requirements are defined, which will be covered in greater detail in Chapter 8.

2. Requirements regarding the scope of the SMS

- No requirements were stated in the previous version of the standard regarding the scope of SMS – that is, the scope of certification. In ISO/IEC 20000:2011 several requirements specify required considerations for the scope of certification such as the geographical locations from which the service provider operates, the customer location(s), and the technology that is being used to deliver the services.

3. **The governance of processes operated by other parties**

- A set of requirements has been added to the new version of the standard addressing processes or parts of processes the service provider is not performing within its own organizational boundaries, but instead has been "outsourced" to another internal or external department and/or organization. While the work may be performed elsewhere the requirements state that the service provider remains accountable for the results and therefore needs to control of (the applicable part of) the process.

4. **The introduction of internal groups**

- The 2011 edition of the standard recognizes the existence of internal groups - groups that are outside the scope of the service provider's SMS, but that are part of the service provider's organization. These are groups with which the service provider will have a documented agreement. This implies that the service provider is required to have clearly defined interfaces with these groups and that the service provider is responsible for monitoring their performance.
- These internal groups contribute to the delivery and the support of the service(s) within the scope of the SMS. This could be for example through the execution of a (portion) of a process (e.g. the monitoring of network components, or the management of storage). These groups can also be the reason for initiating a new service or a change to a service.

B.6   Changes in terms and definitions

A complete list of the ISO/IEC 20000:2011 terms and definitions can be found in the glossary at the end of this pocket guide.

Below we highlight two important new terms and provide some explanatory text.

The Service Management System

An SMS is defined in the standard as a management system to direct and control the Service Management activities of the service provider. According to ISO 9000, a management system is a system to establish policy and objectives to achieve these objectives. And a system is a set of interrelated or interacting elements. The elements that apply to ISO/IEC 20000 are:

* Service management policies
* Objectives
* Processes
* Documentation
* Resources

These interacting elements are required for the design, transition, delivery and improvement of services.

Service requirements

Service requirements are defined in the standard as needs of the customer and the user of the service, including service level requirements, as well as the needs of the service provider. The standard requires that a member of the service provider's top management has the authority and responsibility to ensure that activities are performed to identify, document and fulfill the service requirements. The service requirements are documented in the Service Management Plan. Service requirement fulfillment activities are in essence performed by every process of ISO/IEC 20000.

B.7 New requirements of ISO/IEC 20000-1:2011

When comparing the 2005 and the 2011 edition of the ISO/IEC 20000 standard, the following new requirements stand out for each section of the standard.

Service management system general requirements

Management responsibility
- A list of specific requirements the Service Management policy shall adhere to
- A distinction is made between authorities, responsibilities and management needs to make sure these are determined, assigned, and managed appropriately
- A management representative with the appropriate authority levels shall be appointed by top management who is tasked with fulfilling specific requirements

Governance of processes operated by other parties
- Processes or portions of processes operated by other parties shall be determined
- Even though the processes are operated by other parties, the service provider shall remain the owner of the (portions of the) processes. A list of governance requirements of these processes is given that the service provider shall adhere to
- When a supplier is executing these processes, supplier management shall manage this supplier
- When internal groups are executing these processes, Service Level Management shall manage these groups

Documentation management
- Both documents and records shall be controlled through a series of specific controls as outlined by the standard. This

includes the appropriate responsibility and authority levels to assure the success of these controls

Resource management
- Besides human resources, the standard refers to technical, information and financial resources that are needed to fulfill service requirements, with the aim of developing, implementing, managing and continually improving an SMS that enables meeting these requirements

Establish and review the SMS
- Explicit requirements addressing the scope of the SMS are listed, including knowing what the limitations of the SMS are during the planning phase (Plan) when planning the SMS
- For the executing phase (Do) of the SMS no new requirements have been introduced
- In the Check phase a number of new requirements have been introduced requiring the service provider to perform internal audits; specific requirements are spelled out for these internal audits such as a procedure that is needed describing who is responsible for the execution of such audits and who is accountable
- A series of requirements for management is listed to review the SMS at defined intervals and describes what a review like this should entail

Maintain and improve the SMS
- In the Act phase for improving the SMS several new requirements have been added to proactively prevent nonconformities and to take away identified root causes of nonconformities

Design and transition of new or changed services

Note that the new version of the standard is now clear that this section is one of the "service management processes".

General

- The new version of the standard requires that this process is used for changes with a major impact on a service, multiple services or a customer - (major) projects or programs for example
- In addition, the standard has several requirements addressing the acceptance of the outputs of such major changes

Plan new or changed services

- The requirements for the planning of new or changed services have been enhanced with requirements involving risks and testing
- In addition, requirements around the retirement of services are now included as well as requirements addressing to what extent these new or changed services meet the customer's needs

Design and development of new or changed services

- A series of requirements regarding the design of new or changed services has been added. Examples of these new requirements are dealing the impact these new or changed services have on resources, plans, policies, processes, procedures, documents such as SLAs and service catalogs, and design criteria

Transition of new or changed services

- A new addition is that new or changed services shall be tested and approved before putting the service in production

Service delivery processes

Service Level Management
- The service catalog needs to include the dependencies between the services and components that make up the services
- The service catalog and the SLAs shall be kept up-to-date when implementing changes that affect the service catalog and the SLAs

Service reporting
- This process has not undergone any noticeable changes, other than the new requirement of also generating reports about service complaints

Service continuity and availability requirements
- Additional requirements have been introduced detailing the contents of the service continuity plan(s) and the availability plan(s)

Budgeting and accounting for services
- The process relationships of the service provider's budgeting and accounting for services process and other financial management process in the organization shall be identified and determined

Capacity Management
- The capacity plan also needs to include the consequences on capacity resulting from agreed availability, service continuity and service levels

Information Security Management

- Management is now required to include additional components in the information security policy: security requirements are to be defined, information security risks are to be determined through a defined approach as well as criteria to accept risks, risks are to be frequently assessed, information security is to be audited through internal audits, and, if needed, the outcomes of these audits are to result in improvements
- Also new is that specific information security controls are listed such as the management of risks involving information security
- In addition, the new version of the standard elaborates on what needs to be addressed when assessing a change in information security

Relationship processes

Business Relationship Management

- This process has not undergone any noticeable changes, other than being required to gather information about a response to requirements for new or changed services

Supplier Management

- The new version of the standard is more specific about what needs to be included in a contract between the service provider and the supplier. For example, the interactions between the service provider and the supplier need to be addressed, how the supplier's processes interact with the service provider's SMS, and the responsibilities and authorities of both the service provider and the supplier's representatives

Resolution processes

Incident and Service Request Management

- The service provider is required to have a separate procedure to manage service requests
- The priority of an incident or a service request is based on the impact and urgency of the incident or the service request
- The service provider is required to agree with the customer on the definition of a major incident
- Top management needs to be notified when major incidents occur and make sure that a dedicated person within the service provider's organization is responsible for managing these major incidents
- Major incidents require a review to determine if there is room for improvement

Problem Management

- The service provider is now required to log known errors
- As long as the problem persists instead of the implementation of a permanent fix, the service provider is required to determine how to minimize the impact of the issue on the service

Control processes

Configuration Management

- The service provider is required to frequently audit the Configuration Management Database (CMDB)
- Specific requirements are given on what the service provider is to record in its secure libraries

Change Management
- The change management policy needs to define what constitutes a major change
- Potentially major changes can be the decommissioning of a service and the transfer of a service to a third party
- The service provider is also required to agree with the customer on what constitutes an emergency change

Release and Deployment Management
- The service provider is required to agree with the customer on what constitutes an emergency release
- Releases are now required to be tested before going live; these tests shall be against acceptance criteria, which shall include criteria the customer has agreed to
- Acceptance criteria of a release need to be agreed with the customer and verified by the service provider before going to production
- Unsuccessful releases need to be reversed; further investigation is required to avoid a reoccurrence and identify what improvements are needed.

Appendix C:
ISO/IEC 20000-2:2012

Introduction

In this appendix the ISO/IEC 20000-2:2012 "Guidance on the application of the Service Management System" will be described from a practical interpretation point of view. This informative standard document will not be paraphrased; the reader is encouraged to obtain a copy to benefit most from the information provided in this appendix. Furthermore, the practical interpretation provided here does not attempt to be a full implementation guide. You will need additional materials, information and guidance to ensure the success of your efforts to improve the effectiveness and efficiency of your Service Management System (SMS) based on ISO/IEC 20000.

What you can expect from this appendix is:

1. Guidance on evidentiary documents and records that the standard expects for each section of the standard
2. Guidance based on the ISO/IEC 20000-2 recommendations and based on the author's experience to meet the requirements of the normative portion of the standard, the ISO/IEC 20000-1 document, to generate the required evidence and the road to accomplish certification and to sustain it

To meet these expectations, a standard format is used for each of the 14 processes of the standard; this format is partially based on the format described in the ISO/IEC 20000-2 document.

The ISO/IEC 20000-2 document follows the same chapter naming and numbering convention as can be found in the ISO/IEC 20000-1 document. However, the recommendations providing guidance in ISO/IEC 20000-2 do deviate from the standard's requirements document and introduce additional sub-chapters.

And finally, note that the ISO/IEC 20000-2 document counts almost 800 "should" statements and about 100 additional statements using the words "can" and "may". In other words, this lively document has almost 900 recommendations in support of your efforts of meeting the Service Management System requirements, the "shalls", of the ISO/IEC 20000-1 document. As a result, and since this publication is a Pocket Guide, we have limited ourselves to the most important recommendations.

Service Management System General Requirements (4)

Management Responsibility (4.1)

The Management Responsibility portion of the standard addresses, besides the Leadership principle, every Quality Management principle the ISO/IEC 20000 standard is predicated on. For example,

1. Top management is responsible for involving people and communicating service management goals and objectives (Involvement of People)
2. Service management requirements need to be based on customer and business requirements (Customer Focus)
3. Decisions on priorities about meeting these requirements need to be based on facts such as customer needs, business needs, the service provider's needs and the available resources (Factual Approach to Decision-making)

4. Top management is responsible for putting in place all the prerequisites to plan and establish the Service Management System (System Approach to Management)

Management Commitment (4.1.1)

Examples of evidentiary documents and records to support the requirements are:

- Meeting Minutes about the SMS to ensure its alignment with the business needs
- Top Management Approval Records of the Service Management Policy, the Service Management Objectives and the Service Management Plan
- Service Management Objectives
- Service Management Plan
- Service Management Resource Plan
- Agreed Service Requirements
- Top Management Approval Records of Processes and Procedures
- Top Management Communication Records
- Management Review Meeting Minutes

The Management Commitment chapter addresses the following topics:

- *Top Management Responsibilities*
- *Evidence of Top Management Commitment*
- *Top Management Communications*
- *Service Management Objectives*
- *Service Management Plan*
- *Resources to Support the Service Management Plan*
- *Contents of the Service Requirements*
- *The Role of Top Management in Agreeing and Meeting Service Requirements)*

- *Service Provider's Needs*
- *Conflicting Requirements*
- *Risks to the Service*

The diagram below puts several crucial documents in sequence from a timeline perspective:

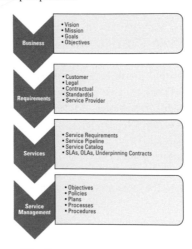

Figure C1 Document timeline

Service Management Policy (4.1.2)

Examples of evidentiary documents and records to support the requirements are:
- Service Management Policy
- Service Management Policy Review Meetings and Minutes
- Service Management Policy Effectiveness Measurements
- Service Management Policy Improvement Actions and Records

The Service Management Policy chapter addresses
the following topics:
* *Guidelines for the Service Management Policy*
* *Improvements and other Changes to the Policy*

The ISO/IEC 20000-2 document elaborates quite extensively
on recommendations for the Service Management Policy. A few
recommendations that stand out are:
1. The policy should be customer-focused
2. The policy should align with the business needs, the business
   objectives and the requirements of the customer
3. The policy should align with the Service Management
   requirements, Service Management plan, and the Service
   Management processes

It is the service provider's responsibility to find the balance
between these customer-based and the service provider-based
recommendations. The better these (sometimes conflicting)
points of views have been documented and the more they have
been discussed with the customer, the better the chances that the
policy will be effective.

Authority, Responsibility and Communication (4.1.3)

Examples of evidentiary documents and records to support the
requirements are:
* Job Descriptions
* RACI Matrices
* Communication Records
* Performance Review Records
* Communication Plan
* Communication Procedures
* Communication Records

The Authority, Responsibility and Communication chapter addresses the following topics:

- *Authority and Responsibility*
- *Communication Procedures*

One of the quality principles the standard is based on refers to "involvement of people". Meeting the requirements of this part of the standard will contribute to higher motivated staff members due to increased levels of involvement in the overall success of the customer, and thus the business, as well as enhanced levels of transparency across the board.

Management Representative (4.1.4)

Examples of evidentiary documents and records to support the requirements are:

- Organizational Chart
- Job Descriptions
- Performance Review Records
- SMS Performance Reports

The Management Representative chapter addresses the following topics:

- *Understanding of Responsibilities*
- *Responsibilities*
- *Asset Management*
- *Reporting by the Management Representative*

The top management representative is responsible for reporting on the value the SMS has delivered to the customer in support of accomplishing its business objectives. The communication between the representative and the service owners of the service within the Service Management scope and the process owners of processes such as Business Relationship Management, Service Level Management and Design and Transition of new or Changed Services is crucial to fulfill this recommendation of ISO/IEC 20000-2.

The diagram below shows an example of an organizational chart positioning the management representative, service owners, process owners and line managers.

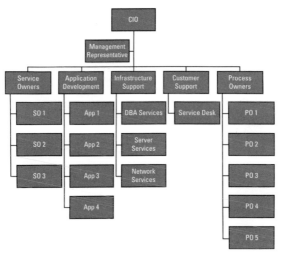

Figure C2 Organizational chart

Governance of Processes Operated by Other Parties (4.2)

Examples of evidentiary documents and records to support the requirements are:

- Service Provider Process and Procedure Documents
- Supplier or Underpinning Contracts with Process Key Performance Indicators

- Operational Level Agreements with Process Key Performance Indicators
- Process and Procedure Performance Records and Reports
- Communication Plan
- Meeting Minutes, Action Item Records
- RACI Diagrams
- Process Improvement Plans and Records

The Governance of Processes Operated by Other Parties chapter addresses the following topics:
- *Guidance on Processes Operated by Other Parties*
- *Other Parties*
- *Demonstration of Accountability and Authority*
- *Process Performance and Compliance*
- *Determining Process Performance and Compliance*

Those processes that are operated by people and entities other than the service provider should be clearly identified, documented and managed as such. It is the service provider's responsibility to demonstrate that it has retained ownership of these processes through appropriate governance measures. This includes a clear description in supplier contracts or Operational Level Agreements of the service provider's and the other party's responsibilities, accountability and authorities. RACI[1] diagrams can be very useful in this effort. In support of creating these RACI diagrams, it might be useful to draw a diagram with all the internal and external parties involved in operating the service management processes.

---

1   RACI is the acronym for Responsible, Accountable, Consulted, and Informed. A RACI diagram identifies the roles responsible and/or accountable for certain activities or tasks as well as who should be consulted and/or informed concerning an activity or task.

The diagram below shows several scenarios of external parties potentially operating processes that are to be governed by the service provider:

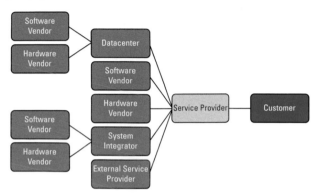

Figure C3 Governance scenarios

Documentation Management (4.3)

Examples of evidentiary documents and records to support the requirements are:

- Document Management Process and Procedures
- Records Management Process and Procedures
- Process Performance Indicators
- Approval Records
- Distribution Records
- History Records

The Documentation Management chapter addresses the following topics:

- *Establish and Maintain Documents*
  - *Documents as Evidence*
  - *Production of Documents, including Records*

- *Control of Documents*
- *Control of Records*

The diagram below shows a high level documentation management process.

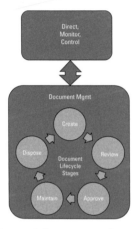

Figure C4 High level documentation management process

Resource Management (4.4)

Provision of Resources (4.4.1)
Examples of evidentiary documents and records to support the requirements are:

- Recruitment Plan
- Personnel Training and Development Plan
- Infrastructure Architecture Plan
- Tooling Plan
- Business Plans

- Service Management Policy and Process Policies
- Service Management Plan and Process Plans
- Budget
- Approval Records of Plans, Policies, and Budget
- Role Guides with Responsibilities, Authorities, Accountability and Competence, Education, Training, Skills and Experience requirements
- RACI Diagrams
- Job Descriptions
- Performance Reviews

The Resource Management chapter addresses the following topics:

- *Provision of Resources*
  - *Resources to Implement the SMS*
  - *Approval of Resources*
- *Human Resources*
  - *General*
  - *Competence, Skills, Training and Experience*

Having the right people on the team is one of the first priorities for Top Management. The "right people" is not only a matter of service provider personnel with the required levels of competencies. Also important are aspects such as attitude (what people think and feel), behavior (what people do) and culture (the accepted way of working).

The diagram below shows the dynamics between Service Management System components and the roles involved in establishing and improving it.

Figure C5 SMS components and roles

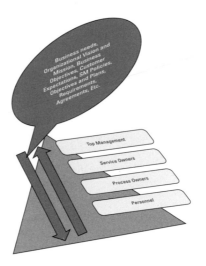

Establish and Improve the SMS (4.5)

Define Scope (4.5.1)

The ISO/IEC 20000-3 "Guidance on Scope Definition and Applicability of ISO/IEC 20000-1" document provides useful guidance on how to define the scope of ISO/IEC 20000 certification. In particular for service providers operating in commercial environments, it is crucial to determine the scope of the SMS. Excluding particular services from the scope may have unwanted commercial consequences.

The diagram below shows some important elements involved
in determining the appropriate scope of ISO/IEC 20000
certification:

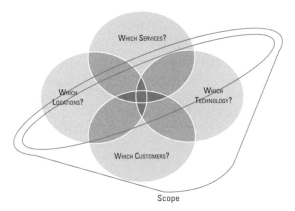

Scope

Figure C6 Scope of ISO/IEC 20000 certification

Plan the SMS (Plan) (4.5.2)

Examples of evidentiary documents and records to support the
requirements are:
- Service Management Plan
- Required Process Plans
- RACI Diagrams
- Process Interface Performance Reports
- Service Management Policy and Process Policies
- Resource Plans
- Risk Management Approach

The Plan the SMS chapter addresses the following topics:
- *Important Planning Aspects*

- *Alignment of Planning and Agreements*
- *Management Roles, Authorities and Responsibilities*
- *Process Interfaces*

The diagram below shows alignment aspects between plans and agreements that are part of the standard:

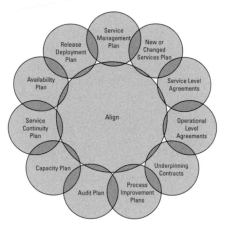

Figure C7 Alignment between plans and agreements

Annex A of the ISO/IEC 20000-2 document provides examples of interfaces between processes and process interfaces with the various components of the SMS. Procedures and work instructions should be very specific about the type, the method, the frequency and the information that flows through these interfaces. Frequent communication between process owners will be necessary to ensure the quality of these interfaces expressed in effectiveness and efficiency metrics.

Implement and Operate the SMS (Do) (4.5.3)

Examples of evidentiary documents and records to support the requirements are:
- Budgets and Profit and Loss Statements
- Role Guides and Job Descriptions
- Risk Management Process and Records
- Process Performance Indicators and Reports

The documented and agreed service management objectives in support of the customer's requirements, needs and expectations should be the driving force when operating the SMS. It is recommended to continuously ensure awareness of these objectives among the interested parties.

Monitor and Review the SMS (Check) (4.5.4)

Examples of evidentiary documents and records to support the requirements are:
- Internal Audit Program, Plan, Procedure and Results
- Management Review Schedule, Decisions, Actions and Results
- Corrective Action Plan, Actions and Progress Records
- Preventive Action Plan, Actions and Progress Records

The Monitor and Review the SMS chapter addresses the following topics:
- *General*
- *Internal Audit*
- *Management Review*

Internal Auditors can benefit from taking into account the guidance that is provided in ISO 19011:2011 "Guidelines for auditing management systems".

The diagram below shows the key questions to be answered when conducting an internal audit:

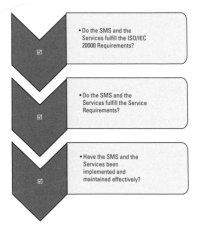

- Do the SMS and the Services fulfill the ISO/IEC 20000 Requirements?

- Do the SMS and the Services fulfill the Service Requirements?

- Have the SMS and the Services been implemented and maintained effectively?

Figure C8 Key questions for internal audit

Management reviews can benefit from the requirements and guidance that are provided in ISO/IEC 15504 Parts 2 and 3 for process assessments.

Maintain and Improve the SMS (Act) (4.5.5)

Examples of evidentiary documents and records to support the requirements are:
- Continual Improvement Policy, Evaluation Criteria, Procedure, Actions Progress Records and Reports
- Approval Records

The Maintain and Improve the SMS chapter addresses the following topics:
- *General*
- *Management of Improvements*

A culture of continual improvement in the service provider's organization is one of the quality principles the standard is based on and is what can make the service provider stand out. Opportunities for improvement should be rewarded and should be given the appropriate level of attention to encourage a continuous allocation of resources to benefit from the improvements made.

The diagram below shows a progression that can be made over time by initially meeting the requirements of the standard and then through continuously making improvements, becoming more effective and eventually more efficient.

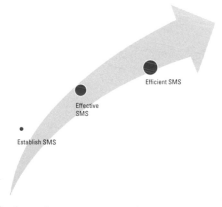

Figure C9 Continuous improvement progression

The subsequent sections of the ISO/IEC 20000-2 document address the 14 processes that are required. Each process is explained through the following five subsections:

1. Intent – explaining the process objective
2. Concepts – explaining process-specific concepts
3. Explanation of Requirements – no further explanation needed
4. Documentation and Records – listing documents and records that should serve as auditable evidence
5. Authorities and Responsibilities – suggesting authorities and responsibilities above and beyond the typical ones for the process owner, the process manager(s) and the process operatives

To avoid the risk of repeating references and descriptions made earlier in this Pocket Guide, the author will refrain from describing each subsequent section. Furthermore, describing the detailed content of the ISO/IEC 20000-2 document would make this booklet no longer a "pocket" guide.

The reader is encouraged to obtain a copy of this highly informative part of the standard.

Annex A

The final portion if the ISO/IEC 20000-2:2012 document lists examples of interfaces between the fourteen processes of the standard and examples of the integration of these processes with the Service Management System. The sample interfaces and integrations will benefit any Service Management improvement effort.

ITIL Books

ISO/IEC 20000

ISO/IEC 20000 - An Introduction
Promoting awareness of the certification for organizations within the IT Service Management environment.

ISBN 978 90 8753 081 5 (english edition)

Implementing ISO/IEC 20000 Certification - The Roadmap
Practical advice, to assist readers through the requirements of the standard, the scoping, the project approach, the certification procedure and management of the certification.

ISBN 978 90 8753 082 2 (english edition)

ISO/IEC 20000:2011 - A Pocket Guide
A quick and accessible guide to the fundamental requirements for corporate certification.

ISBN 978 90 8753 726 5 (english edition)

IT Governance & Risk

Implementing IT Governance

A comprehensive and integrated approach to IT/Business Alignment, Planning, Execution and Governance. This book provides readers with a structured and practical solution using the best of the best principles available today.

ISBN 978 90 8753 119 5 (english edition)

English €39.95 excl tax

Implementing IT Governance
A Pocket Guide

This concise book brings readers the key points to be considered in an IT governance implementation program. It covers the key points and action lists for a sustainable and effective IT governance environment.

ISBN 978 90 8753 216 1 (english edition)

English €15.95 excl tax

Risk Management:
The Open Group Guide

This book brings together The Open Group's set of publications addressing risk management, which have been developed and approved by global experts.

ISBN 978 90 8753 663 3 (english edition)

English €29.95 excl tax

Other leading
ITSM Books

Metrics for IT Service Management

A general guide to the use of metrics as a mechanism to control and steer IT service organizations, with consideration of the design and implementation of metrics in service organizations using industry standard frameworks.

ISBN 978 90 77212 69 1

Metrics for Service Management:
Designing for ITIL

This title is the sister book to the global best-seller Metrics for Service Management. Taking the basics steps described there, this new title describes the context within the ITIL 2011 Lifecycle approach.

ISBN 978 90 8753 648 0 (english edition)

The ITIL® Process Manual

Covers the basic approaches to the fundamental processes – companies will find the concise, practical guidance easy to follow and implement.

ISBN 978 90 8753 650 3 (english edition)

The Service Catalog

Practical guidance on building a service catalog, this title focuses on IT community relationship with the business and users. Including useful templates on key documents such as OLAs and SLAs, this is definitive guide for all those delivering this tool.

ISBN 978 90 8753 571 1 (english edition)